HUMOR IN THE CLASSROOM

ABOUT THE AUTHOR

Deborah J. Hill began her teaching career with a 1971 teaching internship in the Panama Canal Zone. Since that time she has taught romance languages at the elementary, secondary and university levels including adult education, most recently at Ohio State University.

The author is active in the field of international education and has participated in several language study programs in Spain, France, Germany and Mexico. In addition she has led seven student trips to Western Europe, delivering papers on the subject of study abroad at international conferences.

Deborah Hill is an active member of the World Humor and Irony Organization and has delivered papers at their conferences. She is also an award winning member of International Toastmasters and frequently gives talks to various groups on diverse subjects.

HUMOR IN THE CLASSROOM

A Handbook for Teachers
(and Other Entertainers!)

By

DEBORAH J. HILL, PH.D.

CHARLES C THOMAS • PUBLISHER
Springfield • Illinois • U.S.A.

Published and Distributed Throughout the World by

CHARLES C THOMAS • PUBLISHER
2600 South First Street
Springfield, Illinois 62794-9265

© *1988 by* CHARLES C THOMAS • PUBLISHER
ISBN 0-398-05431-2
Library of Congress Catalog Card Number: 87-30420

With THOMAS BOOKS *careful attention is given to all details of manufacturing and design. It is the Publisher's desire to present books that are satisfactory as to their physical qualities and artistic possibilities and appropriate for their particular use.* THOMAS BOOKS *will be true to those laws of quality that assure a good name and good will.*

Printed in the United States of America
Q-R-3

Library of Congress Cataloging in Publication Data

Hill, Deborah J.
    Humor in the classroom : a handbook for teachers (and
other entertainers! / by Deborah J. Hill.
        p.   cm.
    Bibliography: p.
    ISBN 0-398-05431-2
    1. Humor in education. 2. Teacher-student relationships.
3. Teaching. 4. Wit and humor. I. Title.
LB1033.H49   1988
371.1'02'0207--dc19   87-30420
                                                                           CIP

To Bret

INTRODUCTION

MOST PEOPLE would not deny the value of a humorous outlook. Laughter helps us to cope with our fears, to laugh away our anxieties, and to escape for a moment from the rational world. As teachers, laughter can show students our humanity and concern, our flexibility and friendliness. Humor can animate a stagnant class; promote group comradery; and can make even the most rigorous learning enjoyable. Classroom laughter, in a sense, represents the freedom which is at the heart of the American educational system; the freedom to laugh at our beliefs, our institutions, and ourselves.

The purpose of this book is to examine humor and its application in the teaching profession. While many articles on teaching promote the use of humor in the classroom, there is virtually no text on methodology and teachers are usually left to their own devices in developing a laughing relationship with their students.

Another purpose of the book is to help teachers to teach students to laugh. If teachers can teach a student to have a sense of humor about the very serious things in life, they are teaching much more than facts and figures. By teaching students to be able to laugh at themselves, teachers are showing students how to cope in the real world with one of the most important survival skills we have.

It is popularly believed that funny people are born, and not made. This book disputes that myth. It is intended as a "how-to" handbook, relying on the techniques of professional entertainers in order to demonstrate the possibilities humor offers in the classroom.

The humor that teachers use in the classroom is part of the unique and personal skills of the individual teacher. In addition, classroom humor depends on the psychological, social and contextual qualities of a particular class. For this reason, throughout this text I have resisted relaying specific jokes that I have used in the classroom with my students. In the first place, there are many joke anthologies listed in the bibliography that already do that. Instead, *Humor in the Classroom* offers a review of the laughable which combines theory found in an ever-larger collection of humor scholarship, advice from professional entertainers, and practical classroom experience.

Humor in the Classroom is divided into two sections. In Part I, background information is provided as a helpful guide to prepare the teacher to interpret classroom laughter. Part I includes an examination of education-based humor, a survey of the development of the sense of humor, psychological aspects of humor and the social dynamics of laughter.

Part II, concentrates on "how-to" techniques used to create laughter, beginning with language-based humor. Part II also offers specific suggestions on techniques for implementing humor into teaching. Special attention is given to the unique problems presented by test anxiety and class clowns.

Without a doubt, the use of humor in the classroom brings an immeasurable amount of enjoyment to teaching and learning. Teachers who enjoy teaching become better teachers; and students who come to enjoy learning seek out the experience of education instead of avoiding it.

CONTENTS

Page

Introduction vii

PART I
THE MEANING OF LAUGHTER

Chapter One: A SURVEY OF EDUCATION-BASED HUMOR   5
  I. School and Cartoon Humor   5
  II. Education-Based Humor and Television   6
  III. Education-Based Humor in Literature.   7
  IV. Education and Stand-Up Comedy   8
  V. Education-Based Humor in Hollywood Films.   8
  VI. Education on Film as Social Satire 10
  VII. Film Satire and Teacher Stereotypes 11
    (1) The Humorless Bore 12
    (2) The Sarcastic Wit. 13
  VIII. The Student-Teacher Joking Relationship. 15
Chapter Two: THE MEANING OF LAUGHTER: ITS VALUE
                    AND FUNCTION IN THE CLASSROOM 17
  I. The Physiology of Laughter 17
    (1) Voluntary vs. Involuntary Laughter 18
    (2) Natural vs. Stylized Laughter. 18
    (3) The Laughter of Animals 19
  II. The Measurement of Laughter 19
  III. The Value and Function of Humor in the Classroom. 20
    (1) Humor and the Positive Learning Environment 20
    (2) Humor and the Retention of Subject Matter 21
    (3) Humor as Education 21

Page

(4) Humor Promotes Physical Well-Being and Mental Health.... 22
(5) Humor as Socially Acceptable Protest..................... 22
(6) The Appeasement Function of Humor 23
(7) Humor as a Coping Mechanism 23
(8) Humor in a Crisis 24

Chapter Three: THE DEVELOPMENT OF A SENSE OF
            HUMOR 27
    I. Infant Humor 27
   II. Preschool Humor 28
  III. Elementary School Humor 29
   IV. Junior High and High School Humor 32
    V. College and University Humor........................ 33

Chapter Four: WHY DO WE LAUGH? THE PSYCHOLOGY
            OF HUMOR 35
    I. The Origins of Laughter 35
   II. Laughter and Psychoanalysis......................... 36
  III. Laughter and Cognition.............................. 38
   IV. Surprise and Incongruity............................ 39
    V. Superiority... 40
   VI. Personality and Humor Preference.................... 41
  VII. Humor and Intelligence.............................. 42
 VIII. Humor and Creativity 42
   IX. Laughter and Memory................................ 43

Chapter Five: THE SOCIAL DYNAMICS OF LAUGHTER......... 45
    I. The Nature of Groups 45
   II. The Sociology of Joke-Telling 47
  III. Family and Upbringing 47
   IV. Gender Considerations.............................. 48
    V. The Influence of Television 50
   VI. Establishing Joking Relationships.................... 50
  VII. The Meaning of Social Laughter 51
       (1) Greeting 51
       (2) Recognition 52
       (3) Flirting 52

Page

(4) Anxiety/Nervousness/Embarrassment................... 52

(5) Play.. 52

(6) Group Glee... 53

(7) Hostility and Aggression............................... 53

PART II

DEVELOPING A COMIC STYLE

Chapter Six: THE ROLE OF LANGUAGE IN HUMOROUS

           STRUCTURES 57

  I. The Ambiguity of Words.................................. 57

      (1) Homonyms... 59

      (2) Ironic Definitions................................... 59

      (3) Puns... 59

      (4) Oxymoron... 60

      (5) It Goes Without Saying.............................. 60

      (6) Meaning and Syntax 60

      (7) Incomplete Communication 61

  II. Language and Learning.................................. 61

      (1) Tom Swifties....................................... 61

      (2) Secret Languages................................... 62

      (3) Insults and Put-Downs 62

      (4) Comebacks 62

      (5) Learning the History of Words....................... 62

      (6) Foreign Language Learning 63

  III. Colloquial vs. Formal Language......................... 63

      (1) Code Mixing 64

      (2) Slang.. 64

      (3) Jargon... 64

      (4) Taboo Language.................................... 64

  IV. Language and Imitation.................................. 65

      (1) Cliches... 65

      (2) Sayings 65

      (3) Mixed Metaphors 66

      (4) Malapropisms....................................... 66

      (5) Spelling and Misspelling 67

Page

 (6) Impersonations..................................... 67

 (7) The Imitation of Sounds 67

 (8) Mispronunciations................................ 68

     (a) Spoonerisms................................ 68

     (b) Tongue Twisters 68

     (c) Speech Defects............................. 68

     (d) Hyperpronunciation 68

 (9) Humor and Poetry................................ 68

     (a) Lymericks 68

     (b) Graffiti.................................... 69

     (c) Epigrams and Epitaphs 69

(10) Anatomy of a Joke................................ 69

Chapter Seven: THE TEACHER AS ENTERTAINER: COMIC
TECHNIQUE IN THE CLASSROOM 73

I. Learning from Professional Entertainers 73

  (1) Study Popular Humor............................. 73

  (2) Start a Comedy Library 74

  (3) Keep a Joke File................................. 74

  (4) Plan Ahead 74

  (5) Practice Your Jokes 75

  (6) Have Students Sit Evenly About the Room 75

  (7) Use a Joke Cue as a Setup 75

  (8) Be Brief.. 76

  (9) Try Standard Joke Forms 76

(10) Try Writing Your Own Material 76

(11) Construct In-Group Motifs....................... 77

(12) Create Your Own Character...................... 77

(13) Find a "Hook".................................. 78

(14) Use Variety..................................... 78

(15) Be Natural 78

(16) Be Assertive 78

(17) Enliven Your Stories 79

(18) Control Your Voice.............................. 79

(19) Personalize Your Jokes 79

(20) Speak at Your Students' Level.................... 80

(21) Laugh at Yourself Sometimes 80

(22) Help Students Who Don't Understand a Joke 80

(23) Memorize Some "Save" Lines........................... 80

II. What Not to Do 80

    (1) Don't Make Fun of Students............................ 81

    (2) Don't Explain a Punchline 81

    (3) Don't Be Negative 81

    (4) Don't Forget Timing 81

    (5) Don't Make Light of Serious Issues 81

    (6) Don't Tell Currently Popular Jokes 82

    (7) Don't Use Taboo Language 82

    (8) Don't Put Yourself Down as a Joke-Teller 82

    (9) Don't Forget to Relate the Joke/Story to the Lesson 82

    (10) Avoid Ambiguous Messages 82

    (11) Don't Teach Prejudice 83

Chapter Eight: HUMOR AND TEST ANXIETY................... 85

I. Students.. 85

II. Teachers... 86

III. The Test... 87

    (1) Reviewing for the Exam 87

    (2) The Testing Environment............................. 89

    (3) Time Constraints 89

    (4) Pre-Test Joking..................................... 90

    (5) The Test 90

    (6) Returning Exams................................... 91

Chapter Nine: CLASS CLOWNS AND OTHER JOYS OF

        TEACHING...................................... 93

I. The Social Function of the Fool 93

II. Profile of the Class Clown 94

    (1) The Self-Deprecator.................................. 95

    (2) The Hostile Wit 95

    (3) The Mirth-Maker/Social Commentator 96

III. Disciplining the Class Clown............................. 97

    (1) Historical Overview.................................. 97

                                                                    Page

      (2) Teacher Attitudes Towards Clowning 98
      (3) Disciplining the Class Clown 99
      (4) A Special Note to Substitute Teachers 101
Chapter Ten: HUMOR AND CREATIVE DRAMA IN THE
               CLASSROOM 103
   I. The Dartmouth Method 103
  II. Simulation Learning 104
 III. Creative Drama in the Classroom 105
  IV. The Importance of Timing: When to Use Humor 106
      (1) Start Class with a Joke 106
      (2) Use Humor to Get to Know Students' Names 106
      (3) Use Humor to Teach Study Aids 107
      (4) Teach Humor Techniques to Students 107
      (5) Design Humorous Bulletin Boards 107
      (6) Use Humor to Change the Subject 108
      (7) Use Humor in Question/Answer Sessions 108
      (8) Enhance Your Subject Matter with Jokes 108
      (9) Use Humor to Sympathize with Students 109
     (10) Acknowledge Disruptions 109
     (11) Use Humor to Teach the Ignorance Behind Prejudice 109
     (12) End Class with a Joke 109

Appendix A: Selected Teacher/School Films 111
Appendix B: Sample Humor Library 115
References 119

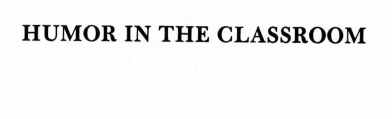

HUMOR IN THE CLASSROOM

PART I
THE MEANING OF LAUGHTER

CHAPTER ONE

A SURVEY OF EDUCATION-BASED HUMOR

EDUCATION is very much represented in the humor of the popular culture. The common experience of school for everyone makes the subject of education a consistent one in cartoons, television programs, in literature, on film, and as part of the standard repertoire of stand-up comics.

The purpose of education-based jokes is multi-faceted. In some cases, making light of the rigors of teaching and learning serves as a means of coping with adversity. In the case of satire, the intention of humor is to expose weakness and folly in the system. In this chapter, we will examine some popular sources of education-based humor. In addition, several recurring themes and stereotypes in education-based social satire will be reviewed.

I. SCHOOL AND CARTOON HUMOR

Many cartoons joke good-naturedly about the hardships of teaching and learning. One of the most popular of these is the *Peanuts* strip of Charles Schulz. School in the *Peanuts* strip is featured entirely from the students' point of view as they face the difficulties encountered during the first years at school. Hardships include the perennial oral reports, test taking, fear of failure, getting into trouble with the principal and the perpetual attempt on the part of the students to avoid studying as much as possible.

Other cartoons offer a humorous perspective of elementary education such as Bill Knowlton's *Grimrose Grammar* which appeared in the *New York Herald Tribune,* and Jeff MacNelly's *Shoe* featuring "Miss Fishbreath." Reaction to classroom activities in *Shoe* are presented from the point of view of a little duck named Skyler. Skyler, like other cartoon students, worries about homework, project deadlines, and poor grades. One of Skyler's unique qualities is his habit of answering test questions whether he knows the answers or not. His incorrect answers are witty, ironic and creative, in addition to being complete fabrications.

Rick Detorie is a cartoonist who presents a humorous portrait of a private elementary school in his illustrated jokebook, *Catholics*. Detorie's cartoons satirize the strict atmosphere of the private religious school characterizing teachers as sadistic nuns.

One of the most unique cartoon treatments of teachers and school is *The Far Side* by Gary Larson. Larson's humor is often black, bizarre and absurd. His classrooms have unusual settings (like the stone age) or take a common occurrence and treat it in an unusual way. In one cartoon, for example, a student's show and tell project consists of a man's head in a jar which teacher and classmates observe as if nothing is amiss.

Tom Batiuk's *Funky Winkerbean* is more specifically devoted to high school humor. One of the main focuses of the strip surrounds the anxieties of Funky Winkerbean, a high school student who worries about girls, grades, competition with other students, and the possibility of failure. This strip also deals with many teacher issues such as competency testing, low salaries, faculty meetings and other trials and tribulations of the teaching profession. Other strips that deal with these issues include Lynn Johnston's *For Better or Worse* and Berke Breathed's *Bloom County*.

Most of the cartoons featured in the *Chronicle of Higher Education* by Vivian S. Hixson and others are related to the pressures faced by professors in university teaching. Common subjects are tenure, faculty meetings, respect and reputation, professional competition, and the pressure to "publish or perish." In *Wake Me When the Semester's Over* Gil Morales offers a humorous outlook of the university experience from the point of view of college students.

Another source of cartoon humor about education is *The New Yorker Magazine*. *The New Yorker* presents school humor particularly from the point of view of parents. Two recurring themes are the "education gap" between parents and their children and fears about the curriculum like new math or sex education.

II. EDUCATION-BASED HUMOR AND TELEVISION

Many children's educational television programs integrate humor into lessons on spelling and counting. The most popular of these include *Captain Kangaroo, Mr. Rogers, Sesame Street* and *The Pee Wee Herman Show*.

In these programs, jokes are told while letters, words, numbers or colors flash across the screen. In some cases, lessons are taught by puppets or through the antics of silly adults or cartoon characters.

Education-based humor is also popular on many evening television programs. Situation comedies which revolve around the classroom have been consistently popular for the last twenty years. In *Room 222* (1969-1974) Lloyd Haynes played the role of an easygoing black history teacher (Pete Dixon) who effectively confronted problems of prejudice, drop-outs and drugs in a big city high school.

Welcome Back, Kotter (1975-1979) was a realistic comedy about a teacher (Gabriel Kaplan) who returned to his Brooklyn high school to teach a difficult remedial class. Gabe Kotter was a teacher who had a healthy joking relationship with his students and a great deal of playful one-liner comedy took place in the classroom. The streetwise students in this series belonged to a gang called the "sweathogs" and included a class yo-yo, Arnold Horshack (Ron Palillo) and playful Vinnie Barbarino (John Travolta).

Since 1986, *Head of the Class* has become a popular school-based sit-com. In this program, Howard Hesseman plays the role of a permanent substitute teacher in a New York City public school. Part of the effectiveness of this substitute teacher is his ability to put the students' academic skills into perspective. Using humor, Hesseman acts as a mentor, guiding his students to become well-rounded citizens instead of one-dimensional intellectuals.

Education-based humor can be found in many situation comedies even though they do not take place in a school. In *Family Ties* (starring Michael J. Fox), *The Bill Cosby Show* and other popular situation comedies which appeal to school aged youths, school is a consistent theme. Jokes are told around the subjects of homework and studying, grades, and success and failure at school.

III. EDUCATION-BASED HUMOR IN LITERATURE

The first literary works that treated the theme of American education tended to be critical accounts of American ignorance written by English visitors to this country. One of the more famous accounts, written by Mrs. Frances Trollope (*Domestic Manners of the Americans*, 1832) was full of tall tales fed to her by early settlers who sensed her gullibility. Such writings served to spread the image of Americans as uneducated whiskey drinking, tobacco chewing, grammar killing wildmen.

One of the educational issues which appears often in literary jokes is related to the issue of the curriculum. While the value of education in America has never been questioned, much humor criticizes the teaching of useless knowledge over critical thinking and the irrelevance of book-learning in the "real world." This anti-intellectual humor is often expressed in jokes based on misspelling. In addition, many jokes laugh at over-educated bores, portrayed as fools outside the classroom, and fair prey to unschooled (but world-wise) con artists.

In the writings of American humorists, the moral of many education-based jokes and tall tales was that it was better to rely on "horse sense" than to fill one's head with a lot of irrelevant facts and figures. This attitude is found in the legends of Daniel Boone and Paul Bunyan and is at the heart of the humorous writings of Charles Farrar Brown (Artemus Ward), and Bret Harte, and in the wit and wisdom of life-experienced reconteurs like Henry Wheeler Shaw (Josh Billings), Mark Twain and Will Rogers.

Twentieth century educational reforms have done much to change the nation's curriculum to offer more relevant courses and to eliminate others which were considered impractical. But social satire about the relevance of the curriculum is still a popular topic.

IV. EDUCATION AND STAND-UP COMEDY

The subject of teachers and education is also part of the repertoire of many stand-up comics. Again, the common experience of the classroom makes the topic of education a popular one. George Carlin, Howie Mandel, Eddie Murphy, Art Buchwald, Erma Bombeck and Bill Cosby, just to name a few, have all made jokes on popular comedy albums about their school experiences or the educational experiences of their children.

V. EDUCATION-BASED HUMOR IN HOLLYWOOD FILMS

Almost from the beginning of filmmaking, the school has had a prominent place in Hollywood films. In serious films (*All Quiet on the Western Front,* 1930; *These Three,* 1936; *Goodbye Mr. Chips,* 1939), school was often an idealized institution where teachers were paragons of virtue and students were something like uncut diamonds, almost perfect except for some needed mentoring from their handsome and caring teachers. At the same time, school satires (*College* with Buster Keaton,

1927; *Pardon Us* with Oliver and Hardy, 1931; and *Horse Feathers* with the Marx Brothers, 1932) made light of the underside of education.

Many famous actors and actresses have played the role of teachers in both serious and humorous films. Ronald Reagan plays a psychology teacher in *Bedtime for Bonzo* (1951); Doris Day is a journalism professor in *Teacher's Pet* (1958); Fred McMurray was Walt Disney's *The Absent Minded Professor* (1960), among many others.

Satirical films about school became especially popular in the 1970s, perhaps a reflection of the nation's general tendency to criticize established institutions in the wake of the Vietnam conflict. The irreverence in films such as *National Lampoon's Animal House* (1974) and *Rock and Roll High* (1979) is typical of the decade's inclination to hold up the educational institution for ever closer scrutiny.

Hollywood films, serious and humorous, offer a unique opportunity to observe the history of education in America. In early films such as *Huckleberry Finn* (Mickey Rooney, 1939) and Hal Roach's *Our Gang* series, teachers teach in one room schoolhouses and the curriculum still centers around literary classics and Latin lessons.

Years later, we can observe how students and teachers on film experience the national identity crisis of the 1960's as American educators reexamined their values and goals. In 1967, Sidney Poitier portrays a black teacher who falls in love with a white woman in *Guess Who's Coming to Dinner.*

Joanne Woodward plays the role of a teacher who is unfulfilled in life in *Rachel, Rachel* (1968). And Dustin Hoffman in *The Graduate* (1967) offers a sometimes humorous portrayal of a student confused about how he wants to spend his life after graduation.

School films, particularly geared to high school age students, have become extremely popular since the late 1970s. This is due in part to the appearance of directors such as John Hughes (*Sixteen Candles,* 1984; *The Breakfast Club,* 1986) and the appearance in Hollywood of several talented young actors known as the "Brat Pack" (Molly Ringwald, Judd Nelson, Emilio Estevez, et al.)

In spite of the many years separating the first Hollywood films which center around the school, the theme of many education-based jokes has been constant. Hollywood continues to find humor in humorless teachers (*Porky's,* 1981, 1983, 1985; *The Breakfast Club,* 1986; *Ferris Bueller's Day Off,* 1986); class clowns and pranksters (Sean Penn in *Fast Times at Ridgemont High,* 1982; Rob Lowe in *Class,* 1983 and

Oxford Blues, 1984; and Rodney Dangerfield in *Back to School,* 1986),
and in the general irreverence of students in the constrained environment of the school.

VI. EDUCATION ON FILM AS SOCIAL SATIRE

Satire uses irony, wit and exaggeration to expose weakness by making fun of qualities which fall below the standards of any ideal. Education is a natural target for satire precisely because the school's standards
are so lofty. Having modeled themselves after the great teachers of antiq-
uity, teachers invite satire, since humor is a natural outcome of perfect
standards in contrast with less than perfect human nature.

Education-based social criticism seeks to expose the weakness of a
school related issue by comparing it to the perfect standard. Ideally, for
example, schools are named after great leaders or presidents who represent the higher goals of the educational institution. Satirical school films
name schools after less than ideal characters like "Lizzie Bordon High"
(*National Lampoon's Class Reunion*) not only to create humor, but to laugh
at an underlying weakness in the goals of the school.

Another target of social satire are school mottos, emblazened in stone
on school buildings and monuments. School mottos are supposed to express the lofty ideals of education. In *Goodbye Mr. Chips,* for example, the
school's dedication sign reads, "To the glory of God and the promotion of
piety and learning." Compare this to the satirical motto at Faber College
in *National Lampoon's Animal House;* "Knowledge is Good." A similarly in-
nane message is inscribed on the walls of Vince Lombardi High in *Rock
and Roll High;* "Winning is Better than Losing."

The topic of the relevancy of the curriculum is a popular topic in
films as it is on television and in humorous literature. In *Ferris Bueller's
Day Off* students skip school and spend the day learning lessons in life.
Ferris admits he is missing a test on social fascism but adds, "That
doesn't change the fact that I don't have a car." Many other films use humor to criticize the relevance of the curriculum including *Teacher's Pet*
(1958), *National Lampoon's Animal House* (1974), *Risky Business* (1983),
Educating Rita (1983), *Porky's II* (1983), *Teachers* (1984) and *Back to School*
(1986).

In *Serial,* a 1980 television satire on yuppies, Martin Mull's wife
threatens to find a job. Martin tells her, "You've got a B.A. in literature.
What are you gonna do? Go door to door and explain the hidden meanings of *Huckleberry Finn?*"

VII. FILM SATIRE AND TEACHER STEREOTYPES

Of all the education-based satire that exists, it is the teacher who is held up most often for humorous scrutiny. Because the teacher ideal calls for teachers with a sense of humor, teachers are often criticized in satire when they have no sense of humor or when they use sarcasm over more healthy forms.

Jokes about teachers and education are possible because of recognizable stereotypes. Stereotypes are oversimplified conventions about a person, group, thing or idea. Originally derived from the Greek word "stereos," meaning "hard" or "solid," the word eventually came to incorporate the idea of the "immovable." Essentially, stereotypes portray multi-dimensional things as static and one-dimensional. The wives of college deans and presidents, for example, are consistently stereotyped as beautiful young hostesses bored with the monotony of their lives.

Stereotypes have both positive and negative functions. On the one hand, by simplifying complex ideas or characteristics, they help to promote an understanding of larger ideas. On the other hand, stereotypes, by their very nature, are often false, inaccurate overgeneralizations which can lead to prejudice and unjust bias.

Whether or not stereotypes are positive or negative in intention or impact, they are nevertheless an important part of the laughable. It is the use of widely recognized stereotypes that makes possible the transmission of humorous ideas about any given subject.

Satirical films tend to criticize teacher types who have no sense of humor or teachers whose sense of humor is primarily sarcastic. While there are many teacher types (such as the new teacher, the coach, or the excessive disciplinarian), in this section we will be primarily concerned with two teacher types which are prominently found in many Hollywood films. These are the "humorless bore" and the "sarcastic wit." In order to better understand these teacher stereotypes it is necessary to study their origins in the beginnings of organized education.

Long before the time of widespread organized education, laughing was associated with sinfulness by church leaders. Typical were the writings of John Chrysostom (cir. 345-407), a man who exerted great influence on Church doctrine. Chrysostom believed that "laughter does not seem to be a sin, but it leads to sin." Others pointed out that there is virtually no mention of saints, prophets or apostles ever laughing in the *Bible*. Beliefs such as these led to the Church position that laughter was unsaintly and something that God or Christ would not do.

Educators eventually inherited Church attitudes because of the direct role that religious centers exerted on the establishment of organized education. During the Middle Ages celibacy and virginity became the Church's expression of the highest good. For centuries, teachers were expected to remain single, essentially married to their teaching jobs. In addition, a Christian standard was established which included a rejection of frivolous associations (including laughter and playfulness).

From the beginning of organized education, commitment to the teaching profession was directly linked to church doctrine. Bodies of dedicated (and unpaid) teachers, most of them associated with the church, participated in a teaching crusade as defenders of the higher cause of religious faith. Laughter in religious classrooms had a limited place, in particular because of its association with disrespect and frivolity.

Most Biblical references to laughter are related to foolish disobedience and disrespect of authority. While it would be an overgeneralization to say that religious bodies of teachers like the Jesuits and the Puritans had no sense of humor, it is well known that they were particularly harsh in cases of laughter citing its irreverent nature in the *Bible* as justification. In protest, popular satire created two primary humorless teacher types; the "humorless bore" and the "sarcastic wit."

(1) THE HUMORLESS BORE. The relationship between laughter and foolishness, dimwittedness and stupidity which was made by early church leaders made laughing an undignified thing for teachers to do. Laughter, in addition to being frivolous, was directly opposed to the image of the ideal teacher as a wise and dignified leader.

Because ideal teachers are supposed to be extraordinary people, satire criticizes (and makes humorous) the boring and ordinary teacher. Perhaps the humorless bore is best exemplified by the character of "Ditto Styles" in the film, *Teachers*. Mr. Styles is an emotionless teacher who has won three consecutive awards for "most orderly teacher." He is so boring, in fact, that when he dies of a heart attack in class one day, his students fail to notice.

Jokes about teachers satirize the humorless teacher by exaggerating their dignity as pride and arrogance. One example of the boring stuffy professor is found in Walt Disney's *The Absent Minded Professor*. Stopped for his erratic driving, the professor resents a police officer's suggestion that he should succumb to a sobriety test which consists of an infantile tongue twister. "I happen to be Professor Ashton, Head of the English

Department at Rutledge College, and a very important person there," he insists. The policeman then orders the professor to recite "Peter Piper picked a peck of pickled peppers."

In *The Piano*, Laurel and Hardy try to deliver a piano to a house on top of a long narrow staircase. After lugging the instrument halfway up the stairs, encountering a number of obstacles on the way, a descending professor insists that they should move aside so he can pass. Oliver suggests the professor should walk around them to which the pompous prof protests, "What! Walk around?!! Me?!!! Professor Theodore Walsh Waschenhaffel, M.D., A.D., D.D.S., F.L.D., F.F.F. and F.!"

The humorless bore is dramatized as having no sense of humor even when they say laughably ignorant things. In *Goodbye Mr. Chips* a teacher arrogantly comments that the "new" H. G. Wells will never amount to much because he is "too fantastic." Similarly, in *Back to School* when a student (Rodney Dangerfield) hires Kurt Vonnegut, Jr. to write a book report on his own book, an English professor (Sally Kellerman) declares pedantically, "Whoever wrote this paper doesn't know a *thing* about Vonnegut." Teacher ignorance (often accompanied by humorless pomposity) is one of the most popular of satirized faults because the ideal requires teachers to be "all knowing" and humble.

(2) THE SARCASTIC WIT. One of the doctrines inherited by teachers from early church leaders included a severe (Old Testament) punishment. In early classrooms laughter was used primarily as a disciplinary tool. Teachers invited derisive laughter from the students, targeting a victim who was called a "dunce."

The word "dunce" is an eponym named after John Duns Scotus, a Franciscan priest who was born around 1265 in Scotland. In reality, Scotus was a renouned scholar who taught at Oxford and the University of Paris. He also founded a school of philosophy which successfully opposed the teachings of St. Thomas Aquinas by the Dominicans, a rival order. Years later, when the teachings of St. Thomas were revived during the Renaissance, those who followed Scotus (called "Dunsmen") were ridiculed as being ignorant.

Eventually all slow learners or ill-prepared students became known as "dunces." One form of punishment required them to wear a hat that came to be known as a "dunce cap." Other forms of ridicule associated students with the jackass. Sometimes, dunce caps included donkey ears; other times, students were required to sit on makeshift wooden jackasses to be ridiculed and laughed at by the other students.

The teacher's role as disciplinarian is frequently exaggerated in satirical films as sadism. Teacher sadists are stereotyped as sarcastic wits who enjoy humiliating their students with negative types of humor such as ridicule and derision.

"Mr. Hand," (Ray Walston), explaining his attendance rules in *Fast Times at Ridgemont High,* warns students, "If you can't make it (to my class), I can make you." When a student (Sean Penn) arrives late, Mr. Hand's humor is sarcastic. "Please come in," he tells the student. "I get so lonely when that third attendance bell rings and all my students aren't here." One of the more famous sarcastic wits on film and television is "Professor Kingsfield" (John Houseman), who portrays a Harvard law professor in *The Paper Chase.*

Some sarcastic teacher types are products of the myth that teachers are people who choose their profession only because they have failed in some other field. This unhappy teacher stereotype is most often typed as an English teacher who really wanted to write a book, but failed to do so.

Katherine Ross plays an unfulfilled schoolteacher in *Butch Cassidy and the Sundance Kid.* She agrees to go to Bolivia with the outlaws saying, "I'm twenty six and I'm a school teacher. And that's the bottom of the pit." Similarly discontented teachers or teachers who are unfulfilled in other major aspects of their lives are found in many other films including *Rachel, Rachel* (Joanne Woodward), *Altered States* (William Hert), *Looking for Mr. Goodbar* (Diane Keaton), *All the Right Moves* (Craig T. Nelson) and *The Breakfast Club* (Paul Gleason).

Typically, sarcastic wits are unhappy with their teaching jobs. "Dr. Bryant" (Michael Caine) in *Educating Rita* is portrayed as a frustrated poet who loathes teaching English literature. Dr. Bryant spends most of his class time daydreaming while mumbling bitterly to himself about his personal problems. Similar types are found in *National Lampoon's Animal House* (Donald Sutherland) and *Looking for Mr. Goodbar* (Alan Feinstein).

Ideal teachers are expected to be the arbitors of fairness. Because they are classroom leaders, they are supposed to have a sense of fairness in their ability to discipline, manage students in the classroom, and in their testing practices. Teacher satire criticizes the teacher and administrator who is excessively harsh and sarcastic in dealing with student behavior.

In *The Breakfast Club,* Mr. Vernon discovers that students have left the library against his express orders. "I may not have caught you this time," he warns, "but you can bet I will . . . I will not be made a fool of." When

Mr. Vernon turns to leave, we see that he has toilet paper hanging from the back of his pants.

Films satirize the teacher who demands excessive control. Sarcastic disciplinarians are characterized as unable to cope with misbehavior in the classroom, expressing their frustration with emotional outbursts which progress to nervous breakdowns and eventual insanity.

In the satirical film *Rock and Roll High,* Miss Togar comes to replace the former principal who has been shipped off to the "funny farm." At the end of the film she herself is led away wearing a white cap and gown and repeating "detention" over and over to herself.

VIII. THE STUDENT-TEACHER JOKING RELATIONSHIP

In this chapter we have seen that laughter in the classroom has acquired some negative associations over the years. Biblical references link laughter with misbehavior and disrespect. In addition, laughter has been associated with ignorance and stupidity, with the undignified, and with a lack of control and credibility.

The use of humor in the classroom is almost entirely at the discretion of the teacher. Teachers can develop a healthy attitude towards humor in the classroom only when they are able to shun the negative associations that classify laughter as mere misbehavior, as wasted time or as causing the loss of face or credibility. It is the teacher who can reject the serious stereotypes perpetuated by the humorous social criticism of the popular culture.

Teachers are in a position to create the kind of learning atmosphere that invites healthy laughter over the humiliating laughter of derision. Only teachers are in a position to encourage the kind of healthy clowning that adds to the sense of group cohesion rather than detracting from it. And only teachers can establish classroom codes of behavior which allow humor to become both a teaching tool and a skill which promotes the enjoyment of learning. In the next chapters we will explore these and other issues and examine techniques which will aid teachers to integrate healthy humor into their classroom learning environment.

SUMMARY

Popular culture has joked about education consistently over the years in cartoons, television situation comedies, literature, stand-up comedy and Hollywood films. Education-based humor serves as a healthy outlet which offers a humorous perspective of the rigors of teaching and learning.

Laughing in the classroom was first associated with sinfulness, disobedience, disrespect for authority and foolishness by early church leaders. In addition, many teachers feared that laughter indicated a lack of control and a loss of credibility. Nevertheless, education-based satire criticizes the humorless teacher, exaggerating their dignity as arrogance and pomposity.

Two common teacher stereotypes satirized in popular films are the "humorless bore" and the "sadistic wit." The humorless bore fears the indignity of being laughed at. The sadistic wit often uses sarcasm to vent hostility about a dissatisfaction with their personal or professional lives. Nevertheless, students continue to prefer a teacher with a sense of humor.

CHAPTER TWO

THE MEANING OF LAUGHTER: ITS VALUE AND FUNCTION IN THE CLASSROOM

MOST PEOPLE think of smiling and laughter as pertaining to a somewhat "universal language." But in spite of the fact that people in every culture express themselves with smiles and laughter, what people mean by these expressions is actually very imprecise.

People have different styles of laughing and smiling. Some are loud, others quiet. Some people gesture while others move very little. Some people cry when they laugh and others do not. Natural laughter ranges from the belly laugh to the thoughtful chuckle, from the cackle to the giggle, from guffaws to hysterics, and from snickers to roars.

Because laughter and smiles are less descriptive than speech, they possess a far greater potential for misunderstanding. Grins, for example, do not always indicate mirth. Grins may be mischievous, guilty, friendly, or nostalgic. Grins in the absence of other gestures sometimes indicate a state of inner peace. And "silly" grins are often associated with ignorance or stupidity. In reality, understanding the meaning of smiles and laughter requires that these expressions be interpreted in conjunction with speech and body language, as well as the social, psychological and contextual factors.

I. THE PHYSIOLOGY OF LAUGHTER

Most researchers consider smiling to be a less intense form of laughing. When we smile, the upper lip is raised and pulled back with a corresponding raising of the corners of the mouth. The mouth may remain closed or the teeth may be exposed as in a broad smile. Creases are formed below and to the sides of the eyes. This causes a slight squeezing of the tear ducks which may release a small amount of fluid into the eyes causing them to "sparkle."

Many muscles and organs are involved as smiles give way to laughter. In addition to the movement of the facial muscles already described in smiling, laughter is more expressive, involving a wider opening of the mouth, sometimes the use of eyebrows, the tongue, and up and down movement of the jaw and most importantly, the use of the vocal cords, which produce a staccato-like sound.

The physical and emotional experience of laughter produces a feeling of arousal or elation. When we laugh, the heart rate accelerates and respiration increases which, in turn, raises oxygen levels in the blood, causing the face to turn red. The level of arousal varies from individual to individual but usually increases with sexual and aggressive joke content or jokes perceived as containing emotionally charged material. Usually, this process is very rapid and most would consider the experience a pleasurable one.

As with smiles, there are different gradations of laughter. Very expressive laughter usually involves a greater amount of body gestures such as holding one's stomach, sometimes rolling on the floor, and in extreme cases, losing control of bladder functions. Violent laughter often includes tearing and louder vocalizations, sometimes in the form of screaming or howling as well as greater convulsions of the diaphragm, producing pain in the abdominal region. This is sometimes expressed as "side-splitting" laughter. The physical response to humor is similar to what occurs when people cry. Sometimes people even cry when they laugh or laugh when they are crying in sadness.

(1) VOLUNTARY VS. INVOLUNTARY LAUGHTER. Some types of smiles and laughter are produced at will. This is called "voluntary" laughter. Laughter is involuntary when disease or drugs force laughter upon the individual.

A fine line exists between voluntary and involuntary laughter. On the one hand, the decision to "give in" to laughter may be voluntary, while that same voluntary laughter can reach an uncontrollable state.

Laughter may be the result of a reflex reaction as when someone is tickled. Individuals respond differently when they are touched, some being more reactive to others at sensitive or "ticklish" areas.

(2) NATURAL VS. STYLIZED LAUGHTER. Some laughter, like speech, is stylized. We recognize that Santa Claus says "ho ho ho," that witches make a high-pitched "he he he," and that an emphatic "a-HA!" can mean "I caught you!" We also sometimes articulate a fake laugh by saying, "ha ha, very funny," to mean, "I don't think that was very amusing."

"Canned" laughter is laughter which is recorded and dubbed over television programs at punchline points. Because people usually laugh more when they are around other laughing people, the motivation behind such laughter is to cause the viewing audience to laugh more at the appropriate points. Since not all of the jokes are "funny" to all viewers, the laugh track let's the audience know that something was *supposed* to be funny.

(3) THE LAUGHTER OF ANIMALS. Most people enjoy watching animals, finding conduct that mirrors human behavior particularly amusing. Many people are convinced that their pets have a sense of humor, indicated by the wagging of a dog's tail or by the similarities of expression in monkeys. However, whether or not animals truly have a sense of humor is an issue of debate among researchers.

Some specialists believe that it is laughter which separates man from animals. They believe that, while animals appear to smile and laugh, the ability to comprehend the absurd requires man's superior intellect.

II. THE MEASUREMENT OF LAUGHTER

Interpretating the meaning of laughter and smiling is a very complex task. In the first place, people laugh at many different things and for very different reasons as we shall see later in this text. Secondly, even if we could be sure about exactly what makes a person laugh, amusement is conveyed by different people in different ways. Some people are loud and overtly expressive, while others prefer to laugh or smile "inside," or "to themselves." Thirdly, smiles and laughter can provide a convincing disguise for a host of feelings which people sometimes prefer to hide. Seeing someone laugh, in other words, is never a guarantee that they are happy or amused.

There are many obstacles to the study of smiling and laughter. Sometimes, people cannot explain why they think something is funny. In other cases, specialists disagree about which jokes or cartoons can be used as a measurement of the sense of humor since there are so many subjective factors in the tester's opinion about what is funny. Despite the many subjective factors surrounding the study of smiles and laughter, experimental psychologists have attempted to measure laughter in order to better understand how it develops and what it means.

There are a number of ways that the sense of humor is measured for evaluation. The laughter of individuals and groups can be examined by using special "Mirth Response Tests." The humor of preschool children is often studied by observation. School-age children can be tested with cartoons or verbal jokes which they rate on a specific scale. Whatever subjective factors exist in the measurement of humor, most tests include problem solving tasks involving an incongruity or absurdity. More attention has been given to verbal and visual humor than to clowning.

The measurement of smiling and laughter is far from an exact science. Different findings may be influenced by the theoretical approach of the psychologist, the disposition of the individual or the group at the time the test is given, or any one of a number of psycho-social variables including personality, gender, and age.

As technology improves, so too will our ability to understand and more accurately interpret smiles and laughter. Recently, for example, experimental psychologists have devised a "Facial Action Code" (FAC) designed to measure precise facial movements and the emotions associated with them. Such technological advances allow for greater precision in the measurement of laughter.

III. THE VALUE AND FUNCTION OF HUMOR IN THE CLASSROOM

(1) HUMOR AND THE POSITIVE LEARNING ENVIRON-MENT. One of the most important functions of humor is to create a positive learning environment. Laughter in the classroom is a sign that students are enjoying learning instead of resisting it as a dull effort demanded of them by adults. Teachers who use humor in their teaching promise enjoyment for students.

On surveys about what makes a good teacher, students consistently say that good teachers, in addition to knowing the subject, make the subject interesting. While humor is no substitute for substance, it is certainly a great enhancer.

Sprinkling lectures with humor makes a textbook come alive. When we interest our students in learning, we teach them to love the process as well as the end product. While you may think that calculus 104 is the hottest thing to hit the geometric universe, your students may find it dullsville. Humor is one way to bridge the gap.

Using humor to boost the morale of the students usually has a positive effect on the business of learning lessons. When students can relate what they learn to a memorable context, whether it is visual or emotional, they are more likely to remember the information. Using jokes and anecdotes to enhance stories provides such an association.

Humor can help create a positive learning environment in which students understand that it is acceptable to make a mistake; even the teacher makes mistakes and is not afraid to admit it or laugh at him or herself. When teachers show they have a sense of humor and aren't afraid to use it, students relax and become listeners. In this respect, laughter can represent a certain amount of freedom from the constraints of the classroom.

Students prefer a smiling and friendly teacher who has a sense of humor. Having a sense of humor is an indication that the teacher is human and can share with the group. This, in turn, encourages a rapport between students and teachers, which is helpful if students are going to listen when adults speak.

When we create a positive learning environment with humor, we open the avenues of communication. Group laughter represents the sharing of a common experience. For a moment, when the class laughs together, people forget their animosities and differences and share in the common experience laughter allows.

(2) HUMOR AND THE RETENTION OF SUBJECT MATTER. Several researchers have studied the effect of humorous lectures on the retention of subject matter. Most specialists agree that humor in the classroom enhances the learning experience, particularly in the case of rote learning. However, humor is not a replacement for repetition as a teaching methodology. And humor has been shown to be most effective when the jokes and anecdotes which supplement a particular lecture are related to the material being taught.

Humor can aid in the comprehension of new material when the addition of a joke or humorous story serves to teach by example. Gratuitous joking does little to help students grasp new concepts or retain lecture material. However, joking that reinforces a lesson can help students remember subject matter by the humorous association. This is especially true in cases of "concept learning" where anecdotes can facilitate comprehension. While explanatory anecdotes do not have to be funny to accomplish the goals of a given lesson, humorous reinforcers are more appealing and more enjoyable.

Subject matter is often reinforced during question and answer periods. A playful atmosphere tends to increase creativity during question and answer periods because students feel freer to express their unique ideas.

(3) HUMOR AS EDUCATION. When students socialize, joking is an important part of their communication. It is in the social situation that students learn the techniques and style of joking as well as what other people consider to be funny.

The subject matter of jokes covers a wide variety of topics. In relaying jokes between themselves, students inevitably pass on some knowledge. Not understanding a joke requires students to explain joke content. This often serves to pass on information about sex, stereotypes, political ideologies, drugs and so forth.

(4) HUMOR PROMOTES PHYSICAL WELL-BEING AND MENTAL HEALTH. Having a good sense of humor has long been associated with physical well-being. In the Middle Ages the word "humor" designated one of the four body fluids, yellow and black bile, blood and phlegm. These humors were used by early physicians to explain people's temperament. When someone had an imbalance in their humors, their behavior tended to be excessive in that aspect of their personality and they were treated accordingly. "Phlegmatic" personalities were lethargic. "Sanguine" indicated jollity. "Melancholy" was explained by the presence of excessive black bile while a "choleric" condition was indicated by anger. While doctors have made great advances in the study of mental health, having a good sense of humor is still considered to be a sign of a healthy mental state.

As described earlier, the physiological process involved in laughter has been measured and studied by experimental psychologists. Whatever approach these specialists use in their measurements, virtually everyone agrees that the experience of humor is not only pleasurable but serves to relieve psychological tensions. When something is perceived as humorous, the body experiences a measurable state of tension and arousal which is relieved by means of laughter. This experience serves to enhance the learning experience as well as relaxing tensions created by classroom constraints.

Specialists in many fields including psychology, education, medicine and business have promoted humor on the basis of its value in fostering good mental health. The classroom environment can be an extremely competitive one and failures there are swift and public. The potential for negative experiences in the classroom is great, particularly for students who are slow learners or who do not conform to the rest of the group in some way. A group that has a healthy sense of humor is more tolerant of failure without getting bogged down in human error and weaknesses.

(5) HUMOR AS SOCIALLY ACCEPTABLE PROTEST. The classroom, for all the good things it represents, is a constrained environment. Teachers have most of the power and control over the students since they give grades, make the rules, decide on matters of curriculum and discipline, and ultimately determine whether or not students will advance to the next level. Such a situation is bound to create some tension. Jokes are often the most socially acceptable way of expressing anger or frustration about school and learning.

Being part of a group requires compromise and conformity on the part of the individual members. It is the teacher who acts as the arbitor of fairness, trying to meet the needs of individual students, while adhering to the goals and needs of the group. Sometimes there is unfairness. Other times there is not enough attention to go around.

Students sometimes feel that class rules are unfair, especially when they see older or younger siblings, friends, parents and teachers indulging where they are forbidden. Joking is a way of relieving some of the anxiety about their desire to have the same freedoms and powers as others.

(6) THE APPEASEMENT FUNCTION OF HUMOR. Humor can help to dissipate a negative or hostile climate in the classroom. The tensions of any classroom can create a potentially confrontational environment. Humor often serves the function of resolving confrontations by making light of issues that a circumstance has made too serious. The sense of humor in the classroom is an important part of the social congeniality of teaching and learning in a constrained environment.

Above all, laughter in the classroom imparts a sense of humanity to students. Teachers who show that they can be the recipients of jokes teach their students to be equally flexible, forgiving and tolerant. Allowing students to laugh at us and with us helps remind them and us that we are human; sometimes right, sometimes wrong, sometimes fair, other times not. But always with an overall sense of pliability coupled with a knowledge and respect for each other.

(7) HUMOR AS A COPING MECHANISM. Family problems, fear of failure, peer pressure, and insecurities about sexuality are only a few of the problems students face as they are growing up. At the same time students often have trouble communicating their fears either because they are afraid of being rejected or ridiculed, afraid that they are alone with their problem, or afraid that communicating with others won't help. Humor is often the outlet students choose to communicate their fears about life and death.

Humor can be a defense mechanism that allows students to express concerns they have about education related issues or about anything they find difficult to cope with directly. Many psychologists believe that students can reduce anxiety about life issues by laughing.

Teachers are usually idealistic people. And the reality of teaching can sometimes be disappointing. This may be due to unrealistic expectations or to the job itself. In some cases, administrators ask teachers to teach a subject they find boring. Sometimes schools lack the funds for preferred textbooks. Other times, teachers must take on so many responsibilities that they have too little time for personal and family life.

Pretending that humor is a solution to these real and serious issues would be naive. But laughter can be an extremely important mechanism to help cope with the realities of the teaching profession.

(8) HUMOR IN A CRISIS. BLACK HUMOR makes use of death, taboo, the awful, and the grotesque to create laughable subjects out of the otherwise unfunny. Black humor is humorous because it causes us to recall our worst fears and to see them in a humorous light. The GARBAGE PATCH KIDS, for example, popularly sold inside packs of bubble gum, use black humor in comic-like drawings of children with their heads exploding or with huge boils and wounds covering their bodies.

SICK JOKES use black humor to laugh at things we should not laugh at. A whole series of "MOMMY MOMMY" jokes use a joke frame in which a child calls for a mother's help, only to have the mother order some unsavory command.

Mommy, mommy. I don't want to eat any more of daddy's brains.
Shut up and keep eating. A mind is a terrible thing to waste.

GRAVEYARD HUMOR is a form of black humor which is primarily concerned with death. Such humor is a coping mechanism against the reality of imminent death. Graveyard humor is sometimes used in geriatric hospitals to help patients cope with their terminal illnesses.

Similarly, CRISIS HUMOR is a form of black humor consisting of jokes about a tragedy, usually told in the wake of the crisis. However awful it is to hear crisis jokes, they serve as an important release of tension created by a tragic situation.

Teachers will probably hear students joking about tragedies that touch the nation such as the crash of the Space Shuttle or the death of an important and beloved political figure or celebrity. But just as some people express grief at a funeral through joke telling, or in the inability to stop laughing, crisis humor is a distancing humor which allows students to not feel the pain of the event. Laughing at a tragedy does not necessarily mean the student is insensitive, disrespectful or cruel. Rather, laughter in many instances of crisis humor is a defense mechanism which allows the mind to cope with the most awful realities of our existence.

SUMMARY

When a person perceives something as funny and derives pleasure from it we say that they have a "sense of humor." But laughter is a complex physiological, psychological and social activity. Because laughter occurs in such a wide variety of situations and for so many reasons, laughter is an ambiguous form of communication. In general, laughter serves as a release of tension to relax us after a situation involving shock or surprise.

People tend to laugh at the incongruous, the unexpected, the unusual, the ridiculous, the ironical or clever. We laugh at nonsense and stupidity, at exaggeration and deformity and at the grotesque. People also laugh because they are happy, relieved or in some cases, when they feel hostile. In addition, laughter can be forced (by some drugs) or faked.

Humor is an important tool in the creation of a positive learning environment. Ultimately, humor in the classroom promotes the enjoyment and effectiveness of teaching and learning and may even be effective in the retention of lecture material. Humor has an important function in the classroom as a coping mechanism for teachers as well as students. Humor is often the most socially acceptable way to express the frustration of teaching and learning.

CHAPTER THREE

THE DEVELOPMENT OF A SENSE
OF HUMOR

I N THIS chapter we will explore general stages in the development of
a sense of humor. Understanding the various stages of humor development will help readers to appreciate how the form and content of jokes
corresponds to the maturation process.

Attempting to assign specific characteristics of laughter by age alone
requires a certain degree of overgeneralization. Readers will note that
most people occasionally regress to more infantile levels of humor development. The popularity of The Three Stooges, the Muppets and comedians like Pee Wee Herman, even among adults, shows that there exists
an ageless quality in the appreciation of what would normally be considered childish forms of humor.

I. INFANT HUMOR

Most child psychologist believe that the first smile appears around
the first to the third week after birth. This smile becomes increasingly
broad as it progresses to laughter in the third or fourth month. In
general, babies who smile early have been found to laugh early as well.
And frequent smilers tend to be frequent laughers.

The first sources of the pleasure expressed by early smiling and
laughter have been associated with the satiation experienced after feed-
ing and the pleasure of discovering a safe environment. Infants also
smile at new objects, funny faces and noises, as long as they are not
frightened by these events. Typically, "peek-a-boo" games and tickling
cause smiling and laughter in the infant's first year.

As more and more information is stored in the infant's memory, smiling occurs in response to recognition of the parents and of familiar

27

objects in the infant's environment. The smiles and laughter experienced by the infant during the first years of life usually come from parents and friends responding to the "cute" things babies do.

II. PRESCHOOL HUMOR

Some of the characteristics of the infant's sense of humor carry over into the preschool years. Preschoolers don't seem to mind getting wet or dirty while playing. And like infants, they may laugh if tickled or if they see a funny face.

Fantasy plays an important role in the humor of young children from approximately the second year through the elementary school years. Children in preschool like to invent objects or scenes and can be perfectly amused in inner play fantasies, humming and talking to themselves as they enjoy their games. Children at this age often enjoy being chased as long as they perceive the activity as playful and safe.

An important aspect of preschool humor includes the imitation of adult behavior in play. This is a fundamental part of the socialization process as children fantasize about their pretend roles as "mommy, daddy," or as they attempt career-related impersonations. Some of the skills acquired in early role-playing games will eventually be used when telling anecdotes at a more mature stage in the development of the sense of humor.

As children develop their language abilities after the second year, they begin to experiment with the sounds of words, sometimes inventing nonsense words or rhyming words with various possibilities. Preschoolers also experiment with their vocal cords, changing pitch, singing words, or trying to speak while making faces. This includes trying to speak while spreading the lips, attempting to speak with fingers in the mouth, or simply speaking while pushing their face in different directions with the hands.

Around age two, children begin to find it humorous to call an object by another name. This is an indication that they are mastering vocabulary and can feel comfortable about playing games with words. At approximately the age of three, children begin to comprehend certain ambiguities in vocabulary and ideas.

Preschoolers like to hear the sounds of cows and chickens and fire engines and take great delight in listening to stories while adults play-act the different voices and noises of the storybook characters.

Because bladder and bowel control is an important issue with preschoolers, they sometimes joke about elimination, laughing about words like "pee pee" or "ca ca." Children most often joke about bowel and bladder functions in order to cope with frustration about their lack of control. As they master these functions, they usually joke less about them.

Preschooler jokes often have funny named characters which facilitate comprehension of the punchline. The funny names may be sexual such as "Mr. Bumhead" or be related to their concern about bowel and bladder control like "Mr. Doody."

As preschoolers learn more vocabulary, they may hear taboo words that they do not understand. How parents react to children when they say taboo words related to sex or bowel functions can influence a child's attitude towards reproducing the taboo words. If parents laugh, the child is more likely to repeat taboo words even when they do not know what they mean.

The jokes of preschoolers are concerned primarily with what is happening to them at a particular moment. When they tell humorous stories, they may ramble, forget part of the information, or include much detail that seems unnecessary. While they talk they can become distracted by whatever activities interest them at the time.

Because preschoolers are uninhibited about mocking other people, their humor is sometimes interpreted as "cruel." In reality, they are too young to understand the impact of what they say to other people. Not until they progress to elementary school do they have the ability to empathize with others.

Preschoolers sometimes laugh at jokes they do not understand. This may be because they want to join in the fun even if they do not know what it means. This is not, however, "polite" laughter. Children usually do not learn to disguise the fact that they do not find something humorous until the age of six or seven.

III. ELEMENTARY SCHOOL HUMOR

As children mature to school age, they may retain some preschool pleasures in their sense of humor. Much of the delight of the elementary school child is derived from playing. This may take the form of fantasy and make believe role playing behavior, playing with toys, board games, bike riding, or ball games and other sports. They may laugh while playing alone or with other children. In their games they are still less concerned about getting wet, muddy and dirty.

Elementary school children usually find amusement in arts and crafts. Most will smile at the finished product at least, proud to have accomplished a beautiful project. Displaying class projects is a source of personal pride for the students and pride often brings a smile to their faces when they have the opportunity to "show off" their work.

Part of the enjoyment of recess and other designated playtimes is the freedom associated with the activity. Announcing playtime to elementary students is always good news and often inspires various forms of cheers like jumping up and down, clapping hands, smiling and laughing. This behavior is often referred to as "group glee."

Elementary school students are generally uninhibited about showing their excitement and delight about a field trip. On the bus they sing "camp" songs, some of which have "sick" lyrics that make everyone laugh. This kind of group amusement must simply be endured by the students who do not care for it. The screams of *100 Bottles of Beer on the Wall* is enough to drive veteran teachers crazy, but it is a great release of energy for the students and indicates a generally good time for most of them.

When elementary school children get together, they may begin to devise or participate in pranks or practical jokes either against other children, family members, or the teacher. The purpose is to embarrass their victim who unwittingly walks into their trap. Children may make a loud noise behind someone's back, pull the seat out from under them, stick gum in their desk, pull a girl's dress up to expose her underpants, or in general, create a disturbance in the new more restrictive classroom environment which makes greater demands for order, obedience and conformity.

Elementary school children enjoy visual humor such as slapstick. A typical Saturday morning cartoon is full of creatures bonking each other on the head or blowing each other up.

Children take great delight in knowing the details about their favorite cartoon characters. They sometimes laugh to hear stories about the funny things some cartoon characters do, especially when the reader is animated.

Elementary school children often find silly adults amusing. They laugh at animated adults during storybook time when adults make funny faces. They laugh at clowns, magicians and other performers. They also enjoy jokes from school visitors like policemen and public speakers who may visit schools for safety programs.

On television, children will laugh at silly adults who sometimes host monster movie programs or other children's shows. Finally, they laugh at puppets who often play the parts of silly adults doing foolish things. In short, children love the opportunity to laugh at silly adults, not only because their behavior is absurd or contrary to adult behavior, but because it gives them an opportunity to laugh at the people who have all the power over their lives.

One of the most outstanding chracteristics of early school humor surrounds children's concern about the new requirements on learning information. Knowing the right answers at school means a reward, while not knowing something can be humiliating. Thus, many jokes during the early years at school show a concern for learning and intelligence.

Elementary school children experiment with newly learned physical dexterity and begin competing with other students. They may cross their eyes, stick out their tongue, try to rub their stomach and their head at the same time, whistle or wiggle their ears, while challenging friends to do the same.

As students master their speech muscles, they find amusement in experimenting with tongue twisters, talking or reading backwards, speaking in secret languages like "Pig Latin," and singing funny songs, including jumprope songs. Often, elementary school jokes are competitive in nature in that one child is able to manipulate the tongue twister better than another.

During the elementary years, children continue acquiring vocabulary and playing with words. One of the most characteristic aspects of this age is that children begin to memorize jokes and riddles. Riddles are especially popular from ages seven to eleven. Many riddles contain latent fears and anxieties about children's preoccupations. One of the motivations for telling a riddle is to prove superior intelligence since the teller knows the answer and proves that the listener is not as smart because they do not.

By the first grade, students have developed what Freud called the "joke facade." This refers to the ability to disguise jokes which have an aggressive or sexual content so that sexual and aggressive messages can be expressed in a socially acceptable way. As elementary school children mature, they become increasingly interested in procreation and sexual intercourse and these subjects eventually become part of their jokes.

During the elementary years, students are socialized to know about existing taboos surrounding the language they are allowed to use with each other and with adults. Also in the elementary years, children learn to feign laughter. Pretending to laugh helps children when they do not want to admit that they do not understand a joke. In addition, most children decide at an early age that they do not want other children to think that they have no sense of humor.

IV. JUNIOR HIGH AND HIGH SCHOOL HUMOR

As students mature, their sense of humor likewise takes on more adult qualities. At the same time, their greater vocabulary and knowledge of life allows them to comprehend and produce more complex jokes. By the time students reach the seventh and eighth grades they usually prefer a more sophisticated humor, losing interest in riddles in favor of anecdotes. Around the time a student enters junior high school their preference for a particular type of humor becomes more firmly established.

Especially, with the onset of puberty in junior high school, students become more interested in reproduction, their own sexual identity, and information about changes in their bodies. Anxiety surrounding these events is the source of much humor throughout life, but particularly true during puberty. That anxiety is often disguised in the form of humor.

Often, anxiety about sex is manifested in homosexual humor, especially among the boys, who may call each other names like "queer," "girl," or accuse each other of masturbating. Joking at the junior high school level may also serve to share sexual information as friends tell jokes which require a knowledge of intercourse and reproduction.

While students have been teasing each other since elementary school or earlier, the "ritual insult" begins to play a greater role in verbal exchanges between rivals at the junior high school level. Opponents try to verbally outsmart each other with insults which imply incest or homosexuality, put down the father's job, or make accusations about the mother's promiscuity.

One of the most characteristic features of adolescent joking is that students begin telling humorous anecdotes taken from real life. By the time students reach junior high and high school, they have become skillful at injecting humor into many social situations. The content of their jokes reflects the concerns of the adolescent student: grades, dating, and eventually, their future careers. Joking during the high school years is a means by which students cope with concerns they have about themselves and the world around them.

As students begin dating during their high school years, laughing and joking becomes an important characteristic of the dating game. Joking in class, for example, may be an attempt to impress fellow classmates and is sometimes a kind of flirting. Accepting a joking relationship may indicate an invitation to friendship or romance.

Sometimes drugs and alcohol are a part of the humorous content of high school humor. A student joking about drugs may alert the teacher that they are drug users. Jokes about drugs refer to the effect of the drug on the brain and the loss of intelligence or refer to the expense of drugs.

If intelligence was important during the elementary school years, it is much more so in junior high and high school since students have had a great deal more experience with grades, parental pressure, and fear of failure. Adolescent jokes attempt to cope with the high anxiety surrounding grades by making light of intelligence, reversing the importance of being smart by making fun of "brainy" students.

V. COLLEGE AND UNIVERSITY HUMOR

While the university student is usually between the ages of 18 and 23, college classrooms often include older students and people from varied backgrounds. This creates a more challenging situation for the professor whose student group is diverse. In addition, college professors have fewer restrictions on joke content since a mature student is more likely to interpret jokes in an adult and contextual manner.

Essentially, college students joke about the fears and concerns they have at this particular juncture in their lives. The humor of college students varies greatly with the age of the student and their familiarity with their environment. In general, freshman are still single and dating, are often insecure about their position at the university and uncertain about their goals at school or in life in general.

If college is a student's first time away from home, students may be experiencing their first search for an identity unique from their high school years. They are probably experiencing roommates for the first time and some are feeling homesick and lost.

Freshmen are also usually excited about new found freedom and are often less disciplined than older students in terms of study habits and classroom behavior. And they may be experiencing the culture shock that eventually comes after too many meals in a cafeteria or too many nights trying to study to the blast of dormitory stereos.

As university students mature, they usually become more goal-oriented, disciplined, and sure of themselves. A small percentage marries during the college years, but many remain single as they experience the good and bad sides of deeper relationships.

Typical concerns of university students include course choice and requirements, fraternities and sororities, dormitory and university life including lessons in university bureaucracy, money worries, and feelings of alienation.

Towards the end of the university studies, students become more pressured about commitments in life. Marriage, career decisions, and the passage into adulthood becomes a foreseeable reality by the senior year. In essence, the sense of humor of the college student, particularly after the initial year, tends to be fully matured.

SUMMARY

It is not possible to describe stages of humor development too specifically because people continue to find delight in relatively childish forms of humor even through adulthood.

In general, the first smile appears a few weeks after birth and laughter occurs when the infant is a few months old. Infants smile as a result of satiation, tickling, and at the discovery of the safe world around them.

As children progress to the preschool years, fantasy begins to play a more important role in their humor development. Preschool children begin imitating adult behavior and experiment with their newly acquired language skills. Some of the jokes told by preschoolers express their concerns about elimination.

By the time children reach elementary school, they are usually less concerned about bowel functions and more aware of the competition expected of them in the learning environment. Children in elementary school experiment with manual and verbal dexterity in their humor.

In junior high and high school the sense of humor becomes more adult-like. Memorized jokes supplement or are replaced by anecdotes taken from real life experiences and adult issues eventually enter into the content of their jokes.

CHAPTER FOUR

WHY DO WE LAUGH?
THE PSYCHOLOGY OF HUMOR

H L. MENCKEN once said, "there is always a well-known solution for every problem . . . neat, plausible and wrong."
Mencken's perspective is particularly relevant to the study of humor and
its causes. Explanations about the roots of laughter have been evolving
at least since the time of the early Greeks. While there has been great
speculation and considerable disagreement over the causes of laughter,
most explanations simply differ in their approaches. The following
pages provide an overview of the best known humor theories. In addition, we will discuss some of the factors related to the psychology of
laughter including personality, intelligence and creativity.

I. THE ORIGINS OF LAUGHTER

Some humor theorists explain the causes of laughter in modern man
by speculating on the origins of laughter in primitive man. According to
evolution theory, man evolved over a period of years, adapting to his environment by developing skills that would facilitate survival. Because
laughter involves a baring of the teeth, it has been suggested that it originated as a defensive gesture against some perceived danger. It is un-
derstandable why some evolutionists might interpret laughter in terms
of its protective function since some forms of laughter are defensive in
nature.

Similarly, some theorize that laughing and weeping originated in
man before he developed a complex language system so that man could
communicate physical and emotional moods.

Some advocates of evolution theory argue that laughter developed
because man, unlike other animals, had no instincts. According to these

writers, laughter was adaptive in that it helped man to cope with painful thoughts (about failure and death) which his superior intellect allowed him to comprehend.

Not all evolutionists believe that laughter had some sort of adaptive function. Charles Darwin, the most famous of these, was unable to explain why laughter originated in man other than as an expression of mere joy. Darwin supported this claim by observing that imbeciles laugh even without any kind of external reasons. Darwin was careful to observe that laughter evolved as a sound that could be distinguished from the sounds made to communicate distress.

In reality, we can only guess about what caused primitive man to begin to laugh. Whether or not laughter developed as a means of defense, as a form of non-verbal communication, or as an expression of mere joy, most evolution theories explain laughter as an adaptive function. Modern man's tendency to laugh may be related to all of these original purposes.

Modern theories about the causes of laughter still tend to take the environment into consideration. One such approach is Abraham Maslow's "hierarchy of priority." According to Maslow, man meets his needs in the following order: (1) physiological needs, (2) safety, (3) love and belonging, (4) esteem, (5) self-actualization, and (6) transcendence. Critics of Maslow's hierarchy point out that people do not always behave according to his list of priorities. Nevertheless, the list is helpful for teachers who will recognize that basic needs usually must be met before students can progress to higher levels of behavior, including the ability to experience playful laughter.

II. LAUGHTER AND PSYCHOANALYSIS

Theories about the psychological processes surrounding humor are frequently explained in psychoanalytic terms. By far the most famous and influential proponent of psychoanalytic explanations of the causes of laughter was Sigmund Freud. Freud's theory of humor is found in his influential book, *Wit and Its Relation to the Unconscious* (1905). In it he notes that jokes (like dreams) contain a latent or hidden meaning which express hostile or sexual urges. The aggressive or sexual meaning behind jokes and dreams would normally be socially unacceptable if expressed without the disguise of humor.

Freud made a distinction between "harmless" and "tendentious" wit. Harmless wit consists of a return to infantile nonsense and absurdity.

This involves a relaxation of mental activity and logical thinking. Tendentious humor is related to disguised or unconscious sexual or aggressive urges. Freud believed that when children begin to perceive taboos surrounding sex and elimination, they develop a "joke facade" which disguises tendentious humor.

According to Freud, individuals are motivated by a life wish which drives them to eat, drink and procreate, and a death wish, which is transferred into aggression. Hostile humor can be explained, in Freudean terms, as a manifestation of this process.

Freud explained that the personality is made up of three systems known as the "id," the "ego" and the "superego." In simple terms, the id consists of the biological needs, the ego controls the psychological and reasoning faculties and the superego sets the social and ethical standards.

The superego is the conglomeration of what the individual comes to believe is right and wrong. According to psychoanalysis, the prohibitions and rewards of the parents cause the child to absorb the parents' ideals and values and thus to learn their system of morality. This, in turn, affects what an individual considers taboo in both the production and appreciation of jokes.

Freud believed that the ability to produce humor and to comprehend it were highly related. He explained that the appreciation of humor is derived from inhibited wishes which are associated with the humorous subject. Psychic energy builds up in psychic channels (cathesix) but is inhibited from being utilized by the superego. The tension is eventually released through laughter.

Forgetting jokes and sometimes not understanding joke content is explained by psychoanalysts as a function of the "Oedipus Complex" and "repression." The Oedipus Complex (developing around ages three to five) designates childhood hostility towards the parent of the same sex and attraction toward the parent of the opposite sex. Repression is the unconscious exclusion of painful impulses, desires or fears from the conscious mind.

Another cause of laughter, according to psychoanalytic theory, is unresolved childhood conflicts. Freud proposed that traumatic childhood experiences led to later fears. Dreams as well as jokes are a key to unconscious thoughts which are revealed in these disguised forms.

In his writings on humor Freud proposed that laughter is a result of released "psychic energy." While psychoanalytic writers may disagree on important details of Freud's theory, they generally agree that laughter is a result of accumulated "tensions" which are released as an expression of inhibited or repressed ideas or feelings, particularly of an aggressive or sexual nature. For this reason, psychoanalytic theories are sometimes referred to as "relief" theories.

Since Freud, many important alterations and interpretations have evolved in psychoanalytic writings. Carl Jung (1875-1961), disagreeing with the sexual pervasiveness of Freud's theories, proposed two dimensions of the unconscious, thus breaking with Freud. The "personal" unconscious consists of material events in a person's life while the "collective unconscious" is a collection of mental patterns shared either by a culture or by mankind.

Within the collective unconscious exist "archetypal" patterns of behavior which recur in myths, fairy tales, dreams and characterizations. One of these archetypes includes a "trickster figure" who serves society as a humorous outlet. Man inherits archytypal or universal patterns of behavior known as "psychic predispositions." According to Jung, a person's appreciation of humor would be a unique combination of experiences in both the personal and the collective unconscious.

III. LAUGHTER AND COGNITION

Cognitive psychologists interpret behavior on the basis of observable behavior as well as how that behavior interacts with the environment. Humor, according to cognitive psychologists, depends on internal processes such as meaning, knowledge, feelings, intentions and expectations and external factors including context and physical circumstances. In order to better understand the role of cognition in explaining the causes of laughter, it is necessary to review the theories of the Swiss psychologist Jean Piaget (1896-1980).

Piaget noted that children mature in genetically determined stages of acquired knowledge. "Cognition" is the process by which that knowledge comes to be known. Children, according to Piaget, reason differently than adults because they are at lower levels in their cognitive growth.

According to Piaget, cognitive development begins at the "prenatal" stage. This includes the physical development from conception to birth. During "infancy," (the period from birth to about 18 months), locomotion is established, social attachments are made and rudimentary language is developed. In "early childhood," (from approximately 18 months to age 6), language becomes well established, sex is typed, group play begins, and the child becomes ready for school. During "late childhood," (ages 6-13), many cognitive processes become adult except in speed of operation. "Adolescence," (ages 13-20), begins with puberty and ends with "maturity." In maturity, the individual achieves the highest level of cognition, becomes independent from parents and engages in sexual relationships.

Cognitive development concerns itself with how children learn rules about the world around them which is necessary to develop a logical understanding of their environment. According to Piaget, children begin their lives as "naive realists," believing everything they see to be reality. This is known as "reality assimilation." When new experiences do not fit or match past information, new information is accommodated or incorporated by the individual.

Eventually, children free themselves from believing all that they perceive is real and they begin to imagine. This is called "fantasy assimilation" which develops during the second year. Children, at this time, participate in "symbolic play," substituting the make-believe for what they know to be real.

Many psychologists believe that the ability to distinguish between reality and fantasy is necessary before children can interpret events as humorous. This ability is seen by cognitive psychologists as a prerequisite to the ability to understand the incongruity of an event and thus to view it as humorous. Children first need to feel confident about reality and how things are supposed to be before they can accept the distortion or falsification of reality, which is part of the humorous event.

As a child develops, knowledge of logical rules, problem solving skills, and the ability to perceive events as humorous becomes increasingly complex. As they build a confidence in the naming of objects, they can feel more confident about renaming things with incongruous and humorous labels. Their ability to conceptualize incongruities eventually achieves new linguistic capacities as their language development progresses. Eventually, children learn that words have multiple and ambiguous meanings and can incorporate this knowledge towards a greater understanding of the complex incongruities which exist in adult humor.

IV. SURPRISE AND INCONGRUITY

Some writers explain the cause of laughter as it relates to surprise. This is particularly important as a child acquires language. Children learn words and meanings from the mother, father and the culture in which they find themselves. A person's peculiar sense of humor can be traced through their characteristic linguistic network. In a humorous exchange, there is a shortcircuiting as the meanings shift. Indeed, the surprise element in the perception of humor is often one of intellectual delight at being "tricked" after the mind has set up a chain of expectations.

The element of surprise is actually a fundamental quality of many humor theories. Freud, for example, emphasized that wit was most effective when it was concisely delivered. According to Gestalt theory, the meaning of a word is determined by the complete meaning of which it is a part. In the telling of a joke, a new element is introduced which causes the complete meaning to be restructured.

One of the most frequently cited causes of laughter is the perception of an incongruity. Something is incongruous when it is interpreted as being in an unusual or unexpected combination with something else. While people do not necessarily laugh just because two things do not correspond logically or harmoniously, in most amusing situations, an incongruity can be discovered. Incongruities come in many shapes and forms but always involve a contrast between an expected and an unexpected image or event.

V. SUPERIORITY

According to some writers, laughter is a result of superior feelings about someone or something which is degraded in a joke. For this reason, superiority theories are sometimes referred to as "derision theories." Laughing at others, according to this theory, makes people feel superior and more comfortable about things they are afraid of such as ignorance, lack of power and control, and excessive behavior. Feeling superior is usually the object of "put-downs" and most jokes about gender, race and religion.

One of the first to write about superiority as a cause of laughter was Plato (427?-347 b.c.). In the *Philebus*, he suggested that we laugh maliciously when we possess superior knowledge over the people we ridicule. Later, Aristotle (384-322 b.c.) proposed that we laugh at people who have an inferior moral character or at people who are more ugly or distorted than ourselves.

Another famous advocate of superiority theory was Thomas Hobbes (1588-1679). In the *Leviathan,* Hobbes wrote the often quoted words that "laughter is nothing but the sudden glory arising from some sudden conception of some eminence in ourself; by comparison with the infirmity of others or with or own formerly."

Some superiority theorists have interpreted laughter as a social corrective. Ben Johnson (1572-1637) believed that the derisive laughter produced during a comedy could correct deviant social behavior in the audience. Similarly, Henri Bergson (1859-1941) wrote that "humor serves the social purpose of castigating unsocial behavior."

Superior laughter is sometimes expressed as the laughter of triumph and victory. When a person or group feels that they have defeated another in some way, their triumph is sometimes expressed with condescending laughter directed at the defeated person or group.

VI. PERSONALITY AND HUMOR PREFERENCE

Laughter, like other behaviors, is internalized by the personal experiences of the individual. Differences in upbringing and life experiences result in the formation of a unique personality. Some people become impulsive, others are careful; some people become optimists, while others are pessimists; some develop a positive self-concept, while others do not like themselves. The mood disposition and unique qualities of an individual's personality effects how people perceive, enjoy and produce humor.

Psychologists sometimes explain personality differences by dividing children into "impulsive" and reflective" types. Studies have shown that these personality types respond differently to humor. Impulsive students tend to have a stronger reaction to humor although they may miss the subtleties of a joke that are perceived by their more reflective classmates. Reflective students often develop a "drier" more intellectual type of humor while the impulsive child prefers clowning behavior.

Other studies have shown that children with a positive self-image develop a stronger sense of humor than those who do not. Children with low self-esteem often display a greater amount of hostility in their jokes.

Personality studies have shown that conservative students are more likely to prefer "safe" humor. Liberals, on the other hand, tend to prefer more risque forms of humor including jokes with a sexual and aggressive content or "sick" jokes.

Another distinction used by psychologists to explain differences in personalities concerns the manner in which people think. "Divergent" thinkers tend to make more unusual associations about events and ideas while "convergent" thinkers do not. Frequent jokers tend to be divergent thinkers.

VII. HUMOR AND INTELLIGENCE

One of the most important factors in the appreciation of humor is the ability to comprehend humorous stimuli. Many psychologists believe that the capacity to distinguish between reality and fantasy is necessary before children can interpret events as humorous.

Between the ages of three and six a child's ability to perceive amusement achieves new linguistic capacities as their language development progresses. Children between these ages enjoy repetitious rhyming and the creation of nonsense words.

Around the age of seven or eight, children become confident enough about what something is called, that they can feel amused about incongruous and humorous labels. This means that they can perceive and find amusing riddles based on homonyms, sequential cartoons, and jokes with greater levels of ambiguity.

From the beginning of the school years students learn that it is important to be "smart." Many of the frustrations surrounding intelligence are hidden in jokes. Put down jokes are just one example of the consequences of an environment in which being smarter than others is so important. Students are often under a great deal of pressure about where they stand intellectually in a group and joking about intelligence is one way to cope with the competitive conditions of group learning.

VIII. HUMOR AND CREATIVITY

"Creativity" is defined as the occurrence of uncommon or unusual, but appropriate, responses. Some psychologists believe that the cognitive processes involved in creating humor are similar to the processes involved in other creative insights. Creative people are usually impulsive, independent, introverted, intuitive and self-accepting and many of them have a heightened sensitivity which is difficult to measure with traditional grading systems. Like other unorthodox manifestations of intelligence, humor is not always recognized as an indication of aptitude since the linguistic genius of wit is simply not measurable.

Some psychologists believe that humor is an expression of creativity or even giftedness. The ability to produce witty remarks reveals an ability to make unusual associations. Sometimes students reveal, through their humorous puns and riddles, an ability to play with language in a more complex way.

Studies have shown that creative children are more playful, are more likely to have imaginary playmates, and generally spend more time amusing themselves with daydreams. Other studies have shown that creative children initiate humor more frequently, understand humor better, and create more humorous material when they invent jokes. Eventually, creative people tend to have a high opinion of others who possess a good sense of humor.

IX. LAUGHTER AND MEMORY

Memory is the mental faculty which allows people to recall the past. Subject recall is sometimes explained in terms of an item's position in the "short term" or the "long term" memory. Repetition is one of the important factors in the positioning of an element in the long term memory where recall is facilitated.

Most jokes enter the short term memory and are quickly forgotten. Time passage quickly causes the factual information in a joke to be eroded or distorted. For this reason, when amateur joketellers retell a joke, it is not as funny as when they themselves heard it because they have omitted or changed key elements. Psychoanalysis would explain the instant memory loss of most jokes as a product of repression.

SUMMARY

There are many theoretical approaches to the study of laughter and its causes. Evolution theory seeks to explain the sense of humor as an adaptive function of primitive man. By far, psychoanalytic explanations of laughter are more prevalent in research literature on the subject. Psychoanalysis, primarily inspired by the writings of Sigmund Freud, explains laughter as a function of repression about unresolved childhood traumas and the Oedipus complex. Laughter usually serves as a release of tension which results from sexual or aggressive urges.

In most cases, something is perceived as humorous when it involves an unexpected incongruity. An incongruity includes anything which is perceived to be in an unusual combination with something else. Superiority of "derision" theory holds that people laugh at something when they feel superior to it.

Other psychological factors which influence the perception and production of humor are personality differences and intelligence. Humor in the classroom is especially related to the process of learning and a student's sense of humor is likely to be influenced by his or her position in the competitive environment of the classroom.

CHAPTER FIVE

THE SOCIAL DYNAMICS OF LAUGHTER

IN PREVIOUS chapters we explored developmental stages and psychological factors which influence an individual's sense of humor. However, students do not live in a vacuum. Social conditions also influence a person's appreciation and production of humor.

In the classroom, students compare themselves to other members of the group in terms of intelligence, age, gender, race, religion, economic class, education level, experiential background and physical features. In addition, students decide whether or not they belong to the group. In this chapter we will discuss the influences of social factors in the appreciation and production of humor.

I. THE NATURE OF GROUPS

Most classroom situations involve a grouping of students with common educational needs and goals. Teaching groups of students is the most efficient way to convey the subject matter required of a school's curriculum. Most groups are governed by a relatively totalitarian government which is based on democratic principles.

When students become part of a class group, it becomes necessary to give up a certain degree of individuality in order to conform to the needs of the group. Students can feel frustrated by the impersonal nature built into most groups, which requires conformity at a time when each member is still discovering their own unique individuality.

In the somewhat restrictive environment of the classroom, students are usually aware of rules and regulations regarding their behavior. From the beginning of the school years, students learn to speak when they are called upon, to follow the commands of the teacher, and to inhibit spontaneous behavior including laughter and physical movement beyond their assigned seats. For this reason, much of the laughter that occurs in the classroom is "suppressive laughter," resulting in spite of its prohibition or perhaps because of it.

As every teacher knows, each group creates its own chemistry. One class of students is gregarious and responsive to humor, while another is sleepy, bored or hostile. A group's sense of humor depends on many factors including physical comfort, interest in the subject matter, the attitude of the teacher, and the time of day. For many reasons, one group may find a joke funny, while another finds it offensive. People, however, tend to feel more comfortable about laughing when they are among friends than when they are with strangers.

People tend to laugh more when they are part of a group than when they are alone. This is the psychology behind the use of laugh tracks on television and the custom of packing people into groups in comedy clubs. Low lighting also tends to facilitate laughter in that people feel more anonymous and less afraid to laugh expressively. Theater audiences, for example, often laugh freely and boisterously at jokes that individual members of the audience might feel too embarrassed to laugh at in another context.

Laughing, like yawning, is "contagious," particularly in a group. There are many reasons why people laugh louder and harder in a group. For one thing, group sanctions allow more freedom to laugh at taboo subjects. In addition, people sometimes laugh at a joke in a group, not because they think the joke is funny, but because having a sense of humor is viewed as socially acceptable. Generally, most people would not want others to know that they did not comprehend a joke. Nevertheless, laughing in a group makes people feel that they are socially accepted and creates a positive feeling of group cohesion and solidarity as a result of a shared emotional experience.

Sometimes, the arrangement of desks in the classroom can affect laughter. In general, students are more inclined to laugh when they do not feel that their behavior is being scrutinized by the other students as when desks are placed in a horseshoe shape. On the other hand, seeing other students laugh may cue students to laugh when they otherwise would not. The position of group members as a factor influencing laughter in the classroom varies from class to class and depends on the unique chemistry of the group.

II. THE SOCIOLOGY OF JOKE-TELLING

Infantile humor is primarily self-centered. During the first years of life babies smile or laugh when satiated, at the attention they receive from others, and as they play and fantasize in discovering the world around them. Around the age of two or three, however, children begin to want to share humor with others. The development of a sense of humor depends to a large extent on the social experiences one has with humor during the early years.

Children learn early that smiles, laughter (and crying) are effective means of achieving their ends. Generally, behavior that is effective, including smiling, laughing or crying, is repeated. In addition, a child's humorous behavior depends on the social models available to them. These social models include family members, television characters and eventually friends.

Preschool children experiment with jokes as they improve their general communication skills. During these early years children have various experiences as new joke tellers and they learn what makes others laugh and what does not. As the child matures, they also begin to understand that being laughed at by others can be a form of hostility and derision.

As students mature, they grow increasingly sensitive about how other people perceive them. Peer pressure becomes increasingly important through junior high and high school. While there is much joking between in-group members throughout adolescence, some students try to avoid joking relationships with adults during this period of their lives.

III. FAMILY AND UPBRINGING

The development of a unique sense of humor is influenced by an individual's upbringing. Parental attitudes about laughter, what they consider to be funny, and whether or not the child has positive or negative experiences with laughter at home, will influence the child's feelings about humor when they get to school.

The way in which parents react to children during toilet training, about the use of taboo words, or the act of children touching themselves or others also influences a child's humor development. Excessive concern about sex and elimination may cause a person to feel threatened by jokes with sexual or scatological content. In some cases, fear and anxiety about something will cause people to not comprehend a joke. On the other hand, sexual, aggressive and scatological jokes provide a socially acceptable outlet for these normally forbidden subjects.

In general, when a child has good social experiences with laughter, he or she is likely to enjoy it and to reproduce it. But when they have bad experiences, they may become overly sensitive to laughter, fearing that they are being laughed at even when this is not true.

Sometimes adults fail to take children seriously, laughing at their attempts to express themselves or making light of their emotions, imitations, or problems. Children can feel frustrated when adults laugh about things that are important to them. In such cases, adults inadvertently cause children to feel shame when they hear laughter that is intended to be loving. At other times, adults may not respond to a child's amusement because they are too busy to share the emotional experience. The multiple humorous experiences a child has as he or she interacts with family members eventually influences the overall humorous or serious attitude towards life.

At first glance, it would appear that a strong sense of humor would be easier to cultivate in a happy home. An environment which is free from conflict would seem to allow a child greater opportunity to enjoy playful states. Ironically, the development of a strong sense of humor often occurs in children from troubled families. Some psychologists explain that humor, in these cases, is used as a defense mechanism to better cope with a difficult family situation. For some children, clowning skills are developed as a way to attract the attention of parents and other adults, particularly in the event of perceived neglect as when there are other siblings.

One of the factors which can affect the sense of humor is the child's position among other siblings in the family. According to some psychologists, first borns would be more inclined to be the most aggressive joke tellers, while the baby of the family would be more likely to be responsive to humor. However, individuals often defy rules and regulations about behavior, rising above a particular family circumstance and developing a strong sense of humor in spite of social factors which would seem to be against it.

IV. GENDER CONSIDERATIONS

Historically, clowning and joking has been dominated by males. In primitive societies, "ritual clowns" were almost always males and many primitive tribes had taboos against female clowns. Similarly, court jesters and traveling comedians were almost always males. Today in professional comedy clubs, there are far more male stand-up comics than females.

Some theorize that joking and clowning has been dominated by males in the past because males are socialized to behave more aggressively while females are taught to behave more passively. Boys, for example, are allowed to be rougher than girls in their play and in general are allowed to avoid punishment to a greater extent.

While boys and girls have the same capacity for the development of a sense of humor, there are some fundamental differences between them. Studies have shown that girls more often take a passive role in a joke telling situation while boys are more aggressive and frequent joke tellers. Because females are usually socialized to be more responsive in social situations, researchers have found that girls are more likely to laugh harder and longer at a humorous event than boys. In addition, girls are less likely to take part in more aggressive forms of joking behavior such as horseplaying and practical joking.

Standards of modesty are more conservative for girls and girls have more restrictions placed on their language, dress, and general behavior. Some studies show that girls are socialized to have a greater need for social approval than boys. As a result of the constraints of modesty and passivity, girls are less likely to engage in joke telling. But while males are aided in the development of a sense of humor by greater aggressive socialization, females are more likely to develop greater language skills which is important for joke telling.

Whether or not an individual derives greater pleasure from jokes which make fun of the opposite sex or their own is a question of individual preference. Some people are highly sensitive to derrogatory gender jokes and others are not. "Sexism," defined as prejudice based on someone's gender, is at the heart of most gender jokes. Sexist humor, like ethnic humor, is intended to put down the other sex by laughing at them.

From a very early age jokes convey sex role stereotypes which has a role in the socialization process. Sex role identity plays a part in determining whether or not people are amused by jokes in which their sex or the opposite sex is victimized or criticized in the joke.

As students become socialized, they begin to understand the behavior expected of their gender and may protest participating in activities they believe to be a threat to that identity. Boys, for example, may not want to play with dolls or may be forbidden by their parents from playing "girl" games. Girls, on the other hand, are not usually encouraged to play with guns or trucks or to participate in aggressive sports.

Sometimes, hostile insults, disguised as "making fun" of a person, attempt to resocialize people who are deviating from their sex role. Calling a girl a "Tom boy," for example, is a term for a girl who is too aggressive;

and the boy, who is not aggressive enough, is called "sissy" or other names implying the boy is weak like a girl. People who are unsure of or sensitive about their sexual identity are most likely to be offended or hurt by sexual accusations.

V. THE INFLUENCE OF TELEVISION

In America, the popularity of comedy in television and other forms of mass entertainment indicates the high value that this culture places on humor. The development of an individual's sense of humor includes absorbing the humor of their particular culture.

The role of television in the humorous socialization of American children cannot be underestimated. Studies have clearly documented that children spend a tremendous number of hours watching television. The entertainment value of humor on television makes comedy programs a large part of kinds of shows that school-aged students watch. In addition to early morning cartoons, programming for young people includes some educational shows and situation comedies.

Canned laughter teaches children when a joke is supposed to be funny. More importantly, television reveals an infinite variety of messages regarding stereotypes about ethnic groups, age and sex roles.

Of more concern to teachers is the prevalence in television situation comedies of sarcastic "put-downs" and "come-backs" put into the mouths of precocious Hollywood children. While linguistic dexterity in the form of clever wit is a desirable social skill, one wonders what television's situation comedies teach school age students about the desirability of sarcasm.

VI. ESTABLISHING JOKING RELATIONSHIPS

Much of the study of "joking relationships" has been done by anthropologists. One of the first and most important of these was A. R. Radcliffe-Brown. According to Radcliffe-Brown, joking serves to pacify hostility between family and non-family members, thus serving as a social control.

Joking relationships occur in many situations and on many levels. The sanction to joke often depends on social context, roles, age and gender, mood disposition, status within the group, and social motivations, intentions and expectations about the outcome of the joking relationship.

Some joking relationships exist between relatively equal peers. Joking that takes place between socially equal friends and acquaintances includes a combination of friendly and hostile teasing and competition. Joking tends to be more hostile as the competition or perceived threat between peers increases.

Another type of joking relationship exists between people of unequal status such as children and parents or students and teachers. Usually, those who have less status in such unequal joking relationships are expected to accept a certain amount of teasing from the more powerful person.

Joking relationships tend to be shunned between people who are supposed to avoid each other. Teenagers, for example, may want to avoid joking with parents; young boys and girls may avoid joking relationships with each other; and social "cliques" may avoid joking relationships with people who are excluded from the group.

Every joking relationship allows specific levels of touching, horseplay, insults, and taboo words and subjects. Crossing the boundaries of these unwritten joke laws is considered socially unacceptable. People of opposite gender, for example, are usually prohibited from using obscenities in front of each other but may do so with members of the same sex.

Most people agree that there is a "time and place" for joking. Usually, group members must agree that the time and place is socially appropriate. Jokes exchanged in the locker room or cafeteria, for example, are usually considered inappropriate in the classroom.

Classroom humor serves as one means to express the group's social control system. Levels of humor permitted by group members, joke content, and permissible levels of hostility and retaliation all indicate information about the group's value system and allowable conduct. In particular, derisive laughter serves as social castigation of unacceptable behavior. Mirthful laughter, on the other hand, can serve as a reward for desirable behavior.

VII. THE MEANING OF SOCIAL LAUGHTER

One of the most common forms of laughter is social laughter. Social laughter occurs in a wide variety of situations as part of the normal process of communication. Laughter is an important part of conversation in that it serves to make group members feel comfortable and enhance the communication experience by making it more enjoyable. In this section we will review the kinds of social smiles and laughter typically used in the classroom.

(1) GREETING. Smiling is one way to greet other people and is usually a sign of welcome and friendliness. The smile of greeting, like

any smile, needs to be interpreted along with other forms of non-verbal communication. The sincerity of a friendly greeting may be associated with a handshake, hug, kiss, or other affirmative behavior while insincerity may be conveyed when people keep a distance or avoid eye contact.

(2) RECOGNITION. People smile when they recognize someone they know and especially when seeing someone in an incongruous or unexpected situation. Seeing someone's picture in the newspaper or on television, or seeing them in a place which is usually out of the normal context of the relationship causes people to smile, regardless of personal feelings about that person.

Often, students respond with a smile when they are referred to by name or when they are singled out for positive forms of special attention or recognition by the teacher.

Smiles of recognition are one way students let each other know when other students are welcomed into their social groups. Not smiling or joking with someone is one way to send a message of social rejection.

(3) FLIRTING. Joking and laughing is an important aspect of flirting. Flirtatious laughter is usually accompanied by other verbal and non-verbal messages including covering the mouth with the hand, whispering to a friend while looking at the object of affection, or even aggressive laughter designed to get the attention of the other person. People who like each other often think the object of their affection is much funnier or wittier than others do.

(4) ANXIETY/NERVOUSNESS/EMBARRASSMENT. Anxious laughter occurs in situations when people feel nervous. Smiling or laughing in uncomfortable situations is a way of trying to cover up the nervousness and to cope with the situation. It is often accompanied by gestures indicating nervousness such as the wringing of the hands, shuffling, blushing, or holding one's arms. Nervous laughter sometimes appears to be fake or forced rather than natural.

(5) PLAY. Play is an important part of the socialization process. When children play together, they learn to work with other people, to abide by rules, to be a "good sport" and to play fair. They also learn to compete, to glory in winning and to cope with failure.

Some play functions as an imitation of adult roles in preparation for later life. Sports and games involve various levels of competition. Sometimes play is simply an enjoyable way to pass leisure time. In other cases, play may be seen as a serious and important activity.

Play is most humorous for students when they understand the activity is just a game and that they can feel safe in participating. The degree to which students laugh as they play is directly related to the level of competition inherent in the game. The higher the level of competition, the less likely students are to feel comfortable about laughing as a sign of their enjoyment about the activity.

(6) GROUP GLEE. Group glee is the laughter which is characteristic of young children at play. Young children often respond to good news (like it's time for recess) with a joy that is accompanied by hand-clapping, screaming, running, jumping up and down, or other expressive actions.

(7) HOSTILITY AND AGGRESSION. Students may also laugh when they have triumphed in some way. This is the laughter expressed in competitive activities. Superior laughter expresses exultation about winning out over some foe, including adversity. As such, it is often very expressive and can include screaming, jumping and aggressive behavior.

Laughing at other people, places, things or events is a form of aggressive behavior designed to advertise the superiority of the laugher. Hostile laughter may express contempt, sarcasm, or hatred. Some researchers believe that hostile laughter reduces hostility while others believe that it arouses aggressive feelings. It is typical of the laughter found between rival individuals or groups.

The hostility experienced between rival teams often gives rise to jokes about the opposing group. These jokes are relatively stylized and formulaic in that they can be told about any rival team by plugging in the name of their school or organization. For example:

Q: What do you call a student from _____ school who has half a
brain?
A: A genius.

Rival jokes almost always insult the intelligence of the rival players. The second most frequent tactic in these jokes is to make fun of the ugliness or supposed immorality of the girls from the rival school. Example:

Q: Do you know why _____ school uses astroturf on their playing
fields?
A: So the cheerleaders won't eat the grass.

OR

Q: What do you call a pretty girl from _____ school?
A: A visitor.

SUMMARY

Humor is very much a social phenomena. The development of a sense of humor depends on social factors such as a child's family and upbringing, television experiences, and gender and sex role identity. Because learning is a group experience, understanding joking relationships among group members is important in the interpretation and production of classroom humor.

Joking is very much affected by the social dynamics of the joking situation. In general, people are more likely to laugh among friends than among strangers. People feel freer about laughing with peers than with people above or below their perceived status. And laughter is more likely to occur in group situations, especially when group members do not feel threatened by joke content.

PART II

DEVELOPING A COMIC STYLE

CHAPTER SIX

THE ROLE OF LANGUAGE IN
HUMOROUS STRUCTURES

TO A GREAT extent, humor is possible because of man's capacity not only to comprehend reality, but to contrast that reality with the impossible. In the real world, for example, elephants and chairs and buses cannot speak, but in the joke world, these suggestions are an accepted part of the playful quality that language allows.

As discussed earlier in this book, determining the reasons why something is considered humorous is a complex and imprecise task. However, it is probably safe to say that much that is considered humorous is so determined on the basis of some linguistic incongruity. Irregular grammar of any variety, inverted syntax, the misuse of tense and mood, or the myriad of humorous devices which make use of inappropriate or unconventional vocabulary words are all potential sources of language-based humor.

In this chapter we will examine how and why language functions as a vehicle for humor by looking at specific conventions used to create the laughable. Readers should remember that where humor is concerned, one person's comedy is another's tragedy. Whether humor is language-based or not, perceiving something as funny depends on the many psychological, sociological and contextual factors already mentioned.

I. THE AMBIGUITY OF WORDS

The language we use in our everyday communication includes a fundamental ambiguity. In order to make ourselves understood, two people clarify potential misunderstandings by means of non-verbal cues as well as questions and answers designed to confirm the speaker's intention.

The communication process used in joking makes use of the basic ambiguity that words and sentences possess. When people expect one meaning and realize the speaker telling a joke meant another, the surprise is potentially humorous. Ambiguity is at the root of the series of jokes that use expressions such as "bankers really count," or "economists have more cents."

DOUBLE ENTENDRE comes from the French expression for "double meaning." The secondary meaning of a double ententre is usually risque. Mae West was one of the most celebrated purveyors of the double entendre, provocatively inviting men to come up and "see" her sometime.

Mistaking the intended meaning of a word, phrase or idea may be intentional or accidental, conscious or unconscious. This is because we do not always say what we mean and we do not always mean what we say (for a variety of social and psychological reasons). A EUPHEMISM, for example, is a word considered to be less offensive than some other term. Most people feel more comfortable when looking for a public bathroom to ask for the "rest room" rather than the "toilet." Saying the wrong thing in a social situation (like calling someone the wrong name) is known as a FAUX PAS.

Because much of what we say is spontaneous, it is sometimes difficult to find the exact wording to express a thought. For this reason, people often say something inadvertently. This is sometimes called a SLIP OF THE TONGUE. A slip of the tongue is popularly referred to as a FREUDIAN SLIP because the unintended expression is believed to reveal unconscious thought processes.

When we speak, the meaning of our words can be both LITERAL or FIGURATIVE. Literal meaning is the surface or primary meaning of a word while figurative language makes use of symbolic meanings, using embellishments such as metaphors or exaggeration. When someone says they are hungry enough to eat a horse, people understand that the "literal" act of eating a horse is meant to be interpreted as a FIGURE OF SPEECH meaning "very hungry." Humor often makes use of the ambiguity created between literal and figurative interpretations of language.

People often use EXAGGERATION and UNDERSTATEMENT to emphasize a condition. We say we are "so tired that we could sleep for a week." Jokes make use of excesses to create humor, especially when the comparison is surprising and unusual.

Of course, it is not merely by words that we speak to others. The use of gestures, body language, facial expressions, clothing, eye contact, and how we represent ourselves generally to listeners and viewers has a great impact on the way our words are received. A fundamental aspect of the ambiguity of language is the often contrary non-verbal messages which accompany speech. It is the great potential for ambiguity that makes language such a perfect vehicle for humor. The following linguistic devices utilize the ambiguity of language to create the laughable.

(1) HOMONYMS. Sometimes humor is a result of the use or misuse of homonyms, words which sound the same but differ in meaning. Homonyms such as "there/they're/their" or "to/too/two" are commonly confused even by adults. The misuse of a homonym is most humorous when the unintended meaning of a sentence conveys something taboo.

(2) IRONIC DEFINITIONS. Many words possess abstract meanings which go beyond the standard dictionary definition. Several humorous dictionaries exist which attempt to expose some deeper truth in the meaning of a word. A typical example is Fisk and Barron's *Official MBA Dictionary* which defines "B.S." as "business school" or "deadwood" as "anyone in your company who is more senior than you are."

Another series of dictionaries creates words for things which have no names. Known as "SNIGLETS," these collections have been compiled by Rich Hall whose contributors come from all over the country. One sniglet defines the adjective "brattled" as "the unsettling feeling, at a stoplight, that the busload of kids that just pulled up beside you is making fun of you." "Floles" are "the extra fourth and fifth holes in notebook paper, created in the hopes that one day mankind will perfect a five ring binder."

(3) PUNS. Puns consist of a "play on words." The unusual or unexpected twist in meaning may be a result of the use of two words that sound similar (homonyms) or the use of words that have similar meanings (synonyms). They vary considerably in quality. Did you hear the one about the psychiatrist who didn't get the job because he was too Jung? Or, the boy who went to Santa Clause High School and graduated in the St. Nick of time?

"Inter-lingual" puns occur when a word in one language sounds similar to a word in another language. Much interlingual humor results from the inadvertent use of a taboo word. Hispanics learning English sometimes mispronounce "sheets"; orientals learning English may say "crapping" instead of "clapping," and so on.

(4) OXYMORON. Oxymoron is the use of opposite terms which would seem to contradict one another such as saying that someone is a "successful failure" or a "rich pauper." The humor, in these cases, comes from the incongruity of such pairings. Saying that someone does not have a single "redeeming vice," or that something is a "definite possibility" can create a humorous ambiguity.

Mark Twain was a master at creating humorous contradictions. On one occasion he advised listeners, "It usually takes more than three weeks to prepare a good impromptu speech." Artemus Ward once said, "Let us be happy and live within our means, even if we have to borrow the money to do it with;" or "No one goes to the theater anymore . . . it's too crowded."

(5) IT GOES WITHOUT SAYING . . . Sometimes humor is created by stating the obvious. One man complained that "the rich people have all the money," and another cliche threatens the listener, "If you kill me, I'll never speak to you again." Sometimes humor is created by stating the obvious in the form of a question as when we ask, "What color is that red bus?" or "How old was that five year old child?"

This kind of obvious statement is not necessarily said with a humorous intention, but such statements can be very funny under the right circumstances. In one case, a man delivering the eulogy at a funeral stated, "He lived his life to the end."

REDUNDANCY is the needless repetition of something that has already been said. While repetition is important to clarify our words, unnecessary redundancy can be very humorous, especially when said under the guise of erudition or greatness. Consider, for example, the immortal words of Calvin Coolidge; "When large numbers of men are unable to find work, unemployment results."

(6) MEANING AND SYNTAX. Incorrect word order sometimes changes the intended meaning of the sentence. This occurs when students (and teachers) write a sentence in which an incorrectly placed clause erroneously attributes action in the sentence to the wrong subject. In the sentence, "One unanswered question is the author of the book," the erroneous word "order" makes the word "question" the subject of the sentence. The sentence should read, "The author of the book is unknown."

One tongue-in-cheek sentence makes use of incorrect syntax to teach a grammar rule that the sentence itself breaks, explaining "A preposition is a terrible thing to end a sentence with."

Sometimes an ambiguous word order is used because the effect is more powerful. We say, for example, that "A mind is a terrible thing to waste." This word order can imply that the mind is a terrible thing. Confusion could be avoided if we said, "It is wasteful (or terrible) not to use a mind." This syntax, however, does not have the same impact as the original version.

(7) **INCOMPLETE COMMUNICATION.** At times, the ambiguity of language is a result of a defect in the communication process itself. Understanding and appreciating a joke requires that all necessary parts of the joke are heard by the listener. A great deal of comedy results from a situation in which only a partial message has been sent or received. Because ignorance is one of the most popular conventions in comedy, it is common to see someone behaving incorrectly because they only know part of the information (while the viewers know more of it).

Blindness and deafness are obvious conventions of comedy because they are the most overt ways to dramatize partial comprehension. Recall, for example, *Saturday Night Live's* Rosanne Rosanna Dana (Gilda Radner) who played a deaf news commentator. Mishearing "busting students" instead of "busing students" or "deaf penalty" rather than "death penalty" resulted in completely inaccurate, and hilarious, editorials.

II. LANGUAGE AND LEARNING

Most people delight in the process of mastering their language. Many word games make use of the amusement that can be derived from this process. HANGMAN and CROSSWORD PUZZLES are just two examples of popular word games that students find humorous. Many amusing language games are designed to challenge students' mastery of their language skills. ANAGRAMS, for example, challenge students to find new words by respelling the letters of a given word or phrase. The letters of "meat" can also spell "team."

The following linguistic devices make use of humor as part of the process of language mastery.

(1) **TOM SWIFTIES.** As students master the parts of speech, they begin to experiment with the possibilities language offers. TOM SWIFTIES are one example of this kind of mastery game. Named after the Tom Swift series of children's books, a Tom Swiftie makes humorous use of adverbs. "I just loved the cheese, she said sharply," or "What a beautiful night, she said darkly," are two examples of Tom Swifties.

(2) **SECRET LANGUAGES.** Especially between the ages of 6 and 11, students enjoy the use of secret languages. Children may create their own language or use an already existing one such as "Pig Latin." In 1979, some students began imitating language used in the popular television series, *Mork and Mindy*. In that program Robin Williams played the role of an alien from another planet who spoke from time to time in his "foreign" tongue. "Nanu nanu," for example, meant "good-bye." Elementary school children enjoy secret languages either for amusement or as a means of privacy.

(3) **INSULTS AND PUT-DOWNS.** Beginning with simple name-calling in the preschool years, children become more adept at verbal abuse as their linguistic skills improve. Typical insults mock the sexuality or virility of the victim or make accusations against parents, particularly the mother's promiscuity and the father's occupation. "Ritual" insults are stylized put-downs especially characteristic of the verbal exchanges which take place between rival gangs. The hurling of insults invites a "comeback."

Hostile REPARTEE and the ability to utilize one's WIT is a respected talent among adults as well. The famous members of the Algonquin Round Table in New York, including Dorothy Parker, Groucho Marx and others, were known for their clever insults and comebacks. Their repartee included QUIPS, TAUNTS, TEASING, or "HALF-SERIOUS REMARKS."

(4) **COMEBACKS.** COMEBACKS are insults given in response to mocking or insulting put-downs. Verbal dueling often takes place in the presence of other students who act as judges about the winner of such contests, repeating stories about the incident throughout the day. Not saying anything is interpreted as losing this contest of linguistic skill.

Insults and comebacks are very much a part of prime-time television situation comedy and more teachers are becoming concerned about this. Television shows often feature children and adults giving "WISECRACKS" and sarcastic answers instead of substantial ones.

(5) **LEARNING THE HISTORY OF WORDS.** Teaching the history of words can be an amusing and informative way to instruct students about the language they use every day. ETYMOLOGY is the study of the history of words and ETYMOLOGIES; available in library reference sections and book stores, are dictionaries which explain these histories.

One way to teach students the meaning behind their words is to explain EPONYMS. The word "eponym" comes from the Greek "eponymous" meaning "given as a name." An eponym is a word that derives its meaning from someone or something. For example, the colloquial student vocabulary word "bogus," meaning "bad" is an eponym derived from nineteenth century counterfeiter named Borghese. In this time of "cultural illiteracy," adding tidbits of information about the etymology of words can convey interesting (and often amusing) facts about history, literature and popular culture.

(6) FOREIGN LANGUAGE LEARNING. Americans sometimes make fun of languages they consider to be primitive or inferior. We refer to something we do not understand as being "Greek" or "Chinese" and Arabic and Eastern block languages, because of their difficult pronunciation, are represented in jokes as mere throat sounds. In many American jokes about foreign languages, French is excessively feminine while German is overly brusque.

Making fun of foreign languages is a way to cope with a fear about not understanding what is being said. Many American students find foreign languages difficult and laughing at them is a way of coping with that difficulty. Because it is culturally important in America to be linguistically dexterous, stumbling over words and not understanding new rules about syntax and grammar can frustrate students who may build up defensive blocks against learning. This often gives rise to ethnic humor about the country and people associated with foreign languages.

III. COLLOQUIAL VS. FORMAL LANGUAGE

The language we use informs the listener of more than the surface meaning of our words. The choice of vocabulary and the way we structure our sentences indicates much about our education and background. And if the listener has a good ear for accents, our speech can be a roadmap to our primary linguistic home.

As we speak, we choose a style that is FORMAL or COLLOQUIAL. Formal language generally involves greater articulation, fewer contractions, and fewer slang expressions. In addition to a more precise pronunciation, formal language chooses euphemistic expressions over base ones and grammatically correct structures over short cuts. Colloquial language does just the opposite. Most speech is not expressed completely formally or colloquially, but in some combination of both forms.

(1) **CODE MIXING.** In general, teachers speak in a language that is more formal than students. Some language-based humor is created when teachers or students speak "above" or "below" their expected language style. Sociolinguists call this "code switching" or "code mixing." Code switching describes an exchange in which styles of language formality are mixed.

Code switching is potentially amusing as when students attempt formality not associated with their age and role. Similarly, when student language is excessively casual in the classroom it is humorous because it contrasts with the formality of the subject and the occasion. Consider, for example, the student who would describe Milton or Spencer as "totally awesome," or "full of it." Or the teacher who advises a student to try "cruising" into a Spanish book instead of cruising down Main Street all afternoon.

(2) **SLANG.** Language is an ever evolving form of communication, particularly in the use of COLLOQUIALISMS. Words like "beatnik," "hippy," "yippy," and "yuppy," all reveal characters of a particular era and the use of an out-of-period expression can be humorous because the speaker shows him or herself to be out of fashion.

Colloquialisms or SLANG EXPRESSIONS are particularly subject to REGIONAL VARIATIONS. Recently, California's "valley girls" have developed a language style that verges on a foreign tongue. Words like "tubular" or expressions such as "gag me with a spoon" may become national colloquialisms among school aged youths or remain peculiar to a particular school or region.

(3) **JARGON.** Jargon is the specialized or technical language of a trade, profession or class. When it is too specialized to be familiar to listeners, the use of jargon sabotages a joke by making important information incomprehensible. However, among specialists, the use of jargon can be an effective way to joke among group members who share a common vocabulary. These are referred to as "IN JOKES."

(4) **TABOO LANGUAGE.** Taboo words and expressions are generally colloquial in nature. Taboo words vary from culture to culture but inevitably, they make reference to sex and elimination. Designating a word "taboo" depends on the speaker and the context of the situation. Taboo words are popular with humorists because of their shocking quality. One of the functions of the clown in society, after all, is the speaking of the unspeakable.

Whether or not we choose to speak formally or colloquially, one cause of laughter is the selection of an unusual word for the one which is considered more common. George Carlin, for example, calls a "Bronx cheer," a "bilabial fricative," a rather esoteric term, one thinks, for a sound usually referred to as a "raspberry." Indeed, the unusual use of language is at the very heart of humor and is part of every one of the following subsections on humorous devices.

IV. LANGUAGE AND IMITATION

When we speak, much of our language is made up of conventional expressions. "How are you," is a standard greeting which is answered with "Fine, thank you." Language-based humor makes use of conventional expressions by subverting the expected.

The laughable is often created by attempting to imitate something's ideal or correct version. The humorous language devices described in this section all make use of IMITATION, especially when copying fails to achieve the perfect, correct or standard form.

(1) CLICHÉS. A cliché is a trite or overused expression. B-Western films often make use of clichés in expressions such as, "Let's head 'em off at the pass."

A CATCHWORD or CATCH PHRASE is an often repeated word or SLOGAN. They may be taken from popular television ads, popular films or celebrity quotes. Examples include questions like, "Where's the beef," (Wendy's), or "Can we talk?" (Joan Rivers). Catchwords and phrases are often temporary and topical.

Another type of cliché is the MOMILY, defined as "expressions mothers overuse." Examples are "Don't cross your eyes or they'll stay like that," or "If I've told you once I've told you a hundred times . . ." Clichés are a common convention in the creation of humor because they are highly recognized standard expressions which can be easily altered or placed out of context.

(2) SAYINGS. ADAGES, MAXIMES, BYWORDS, SAYINGS and PROVERBS are conventionalized phrases containing words of wisdom. We say, for example, that "It is better to give than to receive," or, "A rolling stone gathers no moss." Sayings can be humorous when they incorrectly attempt to quote the correct version such as, "It is better to give a rolling stone than to receive moss."

Usually, the use of sayings requires that the listener recognizes the correct or ideal saying in order to appreciate how the mistake contrasts (humorously) with it. A whole category of jokes take advantage of this language convention as the following joke illustrates.

Once there was an African king who was worried someone might steal his throne. For this reason, he hid the huge chair in his attic. One day, while sitting in his grass hut, the throne came crashing onto his head and killed him. The moral of the story? People who live in grass houses shouldn't stow thrones.

APHORISMS are relatively aristocratic maxims which state some universal principle, often with some irony. The following aphorism by Remy de Gourmont (1858-1915), the French poet, critic and novelist, is illustrative:

We live less and less and learn more and more. I have seen a man laughed at for examining a dead leaf attentively and with pleasure. No one would have laughed to hear a string of botanical terms muttered over it.

(3) MIXED METAPHORS. Another humorous language convention is the mixed metaphor. A metaphor is a figure of speech in which the meaning of something is transformed from the object it usually designates to another idea in order to create a new and unusual comparison. We may say, for example, that young people are in the "spring" of their lives or that the elderly are in the "winter" of their lives. Taking two metaphors and mixing their words and meanings can be humorous when it exposes that the speaker (or writer) does not understand the meaning of the phrases. In this case, the humor is derived from an attempt to imitate the correct metaphor. For example, when someone has a positive view of life we say that they "see the world through rose colored glasses." Then there was the man who said about the best year of his life that he was "drinking out of rose colored glasses."

Similarly, people sometimes MISQUOTE SAYINGS which contain metaphors. For example, instead of saying, "That's just water over the dam," or "That's just water under the bridge," someone might say, "That's just water under the dam," or "over the bridge."

(4) MALAPROPISMS. A malapropism involves the mistaken use of a word which sounds similar to the correct one. It was so named for an English travel writer, Mrs. Malaprop from the comedy, *The Rivals* by Richard Brinsley Sheridan. Mrs. Malaprop often misinterpreted things she heard and saw while traveling in America. It was a favorite device used on the Archie Bunker show to reveal Archie's ignorance and prejudice.

Malapropisms result from inadequate understanding of a word coupled with a desire to impress. There was the man, for example, accused of "bigotry" who replied indignantly, "I resemble that remark." In order for a malapropism to be perceived as humorous, it is usually necessary for the listener to understand the linguistic error.

(5) SPELLING AND MISSPELLING. American humor writers have established a tradition of spelling-related jokes. One of the most famous was Charles Farrar Browne (1834-1867), better known under his pseudonym, Artemus Ward. His series of letters were supposedly written by a carnival manager who commented on current events in New England dialect. Typical of this tradition was an excuse note written by a student who claimed he could not come to school because he had "new monia." Other typical misspellings are "raindear" or "Catholick."

Misspellings, often the result of TYPOS (typographical errors) are usually more humorous if the new and incorrect spelling somehow changes the original meaning of the sentence like changing "importance" to "impotence" or "friend" to "fiend." In one case a grant from the Coca-Cola Foundation was listed in a college newspaper under "Scholarsips."

(6) IMPERSONATIONS. Imitation jokes exaggerate a person's most outstanding features, often for the purpose of ridicule. Jokes which are acted out include IMPERSONATIONS, CARICATURES, PARODIES or SATIRES which may take several forms.

People usually find it humorous to watch others imitating someone or something, especially when the impersonation is well done. Impersonations are a favorite act in professional comedy. In addition, tongue-in-cheek celebrity look-alike contests are popular in America.

(7) THE IMITATION OF SOUNDS. Professional comics teach us that certain sounds (such as words that contain the "k" sound) are funnier than others. Most people recognize that some words, even though they mean almost the same thing as another word, make people laugh more. "Buick" sounds funnier than "Chevrolet," and "wimp" sounds funnier than "timid."

Sounds may be considered funny because they are heard out of the expected context. We expect to hear a horse in a barn or on a farm, but not in a school gymnasium. We anticipate classroom sounds, but school noises do not include popular student noises like Hawaiian love calls and jungle sounds. Any sound not normally associated with expected or appropriate classroom noises can be a source of humor as any teacher well knows.

Some words "sound" funny as a result of ONOMATOPEIA, a word that sounds like its referent such as "cuckoo, buzz, snap, crack, whoosh, moo," or "boom." Onomatopeia is sometimes created with the repetition of vowels or consonants in a sentence, and the sound can be humorous.

(8) MISPRONUNCIATIONS. The mispronunciation of words may take one of several forms. Sometimes it is simply a question of a "SLIP OF THE TONGUE."

(a) Spoonerisms are accidental inversions and are particularly funny when the inversion causes one to say something taboo. Spoonerisms were named after William A. Spooner, Dean of New College in Oxford, a man who was known for his slips of the tongue. It involves the transposition of sounds, letters, words or phrases creating a new and inappropriate meaning like the usher who wanted to say, "Let me show you to your seat," but said, "Let me sew you to your sheet."

(b) Tongue Twisters are groups of words of phonetic similarity which stress the speech aparatus if attempted in rapid succession. The purpose of many of them is to cause the speaker to say something taboo. Others, like "Unique New York," are simply difficult to articulate.

(c) Speech Defects are sometimes laughed at or imitated as a humorous device. Pretending not to be able to control the speech apparatus by a twisting of the mouth or holding one's nose to create a nasal voice are examples of devices students may find humorous while experimenting with their newly developing language skills.

Making fun of someone with a real speech defect can be a distancing device used to hide fears about speech handicaps. Like all jokes about defects in others, laughing at someone with a speech defect can also be an expression of superiority.

(d) Hyperpronunciation involves the exaggerated pronunciation of a word. In some cases, hyperpronunciations betray pomposity as when someone who pronounces "tomato" and "aunt" with a short "a" then mispronounces "potatoe" using the same rule.

Mispronouncing a word, even if it is used correctly in the sentence, can betray the speaker's ignorance or pomposity and is thus potentially humorous.

(9) HUMOR AND POETRY. One of the challenging and sometimes fun qualities of language is its ability to conform to standard poetic formats. This requires a certain amount of ingenuity on the part of the student who must fashion his or her poem to predetermined rules of rhyme and meter. Probably the most prolific forms of student poetry are the lymerick and short verse found in the form of graffiti.

(a) Lymericks. Lymericks treat almost any subject and there are several large collections of them. As poetry goes, they are relatively easy to create and very popular with elementary school children experimenting with their creative language abilities. Here is an example:

An old man from Kalamazoo
Once dreamed he was eating his shoe
    He awoke late that night
    In a terrible fright
Now instead of one tongue, he has two

(b) Graffiti. Graffiti found primarily on bathroom walls often contains scatological or sexual reference and sometimes takes on multiple anonymous authorship. However, graffiti does not limit its topics exclusively to bathroom humor and taboo words, nor its form of poetry. Witticisms, comments on the irony of life and even some social criticism can likewise be found in this often humorous language form.

The following poem imitates or parodies a well known model. Observe how it is humorous precisely because it fails to meet the higher standards of its predecessor's ideal and because it dares to mock a relatively sacred genre by lauding a subject much baser than the original.

I think that I shall never hear
a poem as lovely as a beer.
That good ol' brew tastes best on tap
with its golden base and snowy cap.
That lovely stuff I drink all day
until my memory melts away.
Poems are made by fools I fear,
but only Schlitz can make a beer.
OSU LIBRARY

(c) Epigrams and Epitaphs. An EPIGRAM is a short poem or saying expressing a single thought with terseness and wit.

Three things must epigrams like bees, have all,
A sting, and honey, and a body small.

Epigrams can also be concise and cleverly worded statements such as "Foxhunting is the pursuit of the uneatable by the unspeakable."

Similarly, EPITAPHS are short poems written on tombstones. Typically they begin, "Here lies," and in joke version, include a humorous poem about the deceased.

(10) ANATOMY OF A JOKE. Most of the humorous language devices discussed in this chapter are generically referred to as "jokes." While jokes come in many shapes and sizes, they all do about the same thing. In general, jokes are patterned constructions which set the listener up for a response, but quickly subvert what is expected with an alternate meaning in the form of a PUNCHLINE.

Setups are crucial to joke formats. In fact, jokes work precisely because the thought processes which follow any setup are predictable.

Jokes take advantage of the expected by delivering something unexpected. This is called "SWITCHING." Take the following example:

> SETUP: Last night I had a dream I was in a boat with Dolly Parton.
>   Oh really? How did it go?
> PUNCHLINE: Great! I caught a ten pound bass.

Most listeners recognize immediately that an unusual and humorous response is expected after a joke setup. Some jokes take advantage of this expectation by switching a humorous punchline for a serious one. Perhaps this is best illustrated with one of the oldest jokes in the world, "Why did the chicken cross the road?" Once the setup is perceived, the listener begins looking for a twist or a surprise answer. No one expects the answer to be serious and logical. Thus, in the rare event someone has not already fallen for this joke, when they are told that the chicken crosses the road to get to the other side the surprise element is still intact.

Taking this process of expectation one step further, some joke setups lead the listener to believe they are hearing an "old" joke, but switch the expected standard setup. In the case of "Why did the chicken cross the road," everyone expects to hear, "to get to the other side." Typical switches include absurd answers like, "because his mother told him to," or "because that's where the busstop was."

Usually, once you have a listener in a joking frame of mind, it is easier to increase the playfulness of communication. Many elephant jokes capitalize on this fact in that each joke is not particularly funny in itself, but told in a string of half a dozen jokes they can become funnier because of the increasing absurdity.

Some jokes which are mildly humorous are intentionally used as setups for much funnier jokes. This is especially true when professional comedians tell a long string of jokes, each one building to a final joke that serves as the punchline for the set.

Sometimes the functions of the SETUP is to cue the listener that a playful speech event is taking place. Thus, when someone asks "Do you know how many teachers it takes to screw in a lightbulb?" or "What did the elephants say when they were coming over the mountain?" we do not question the relevance of the riddle in the reality of the situation in which they occur.

Not all setups cue the listener to a playful speech event. Telephone prank setups, for example, lead the victim to believe that the speech event is a serious one. Telephone pranks beg a normal response to a simple question, then "switch" the expected reply. Example:

SETUP: Is your refrigerator running?
STANDARD ANSWER: Yes, I think so.
SWITCH: Then you'd better go catch it.

The popularity of RIDDLES in our society is a reflection of the pressure students begin to feel about knowing facts, especially after they enter school. Telling riddles is an intellectual challenge and solving them can be relatively satisfying to the young language learner.

Riddles are jokes which pose questions that do not seem to have any logical answer. "Why," one riddle asks, "are brides unlucky on their wedding day?" Since wedding days are supposed to be happy and lucky occasions, the solution appears to be impossible. The response? Brides are unlucky because they never get to marry the "best" man.

Because riddles are most often language based, the puzzle presented has its roots in the ambiguity of words and phrases. Riddle ambiguity may be lexical (as when a single word has two meanings); phonological (as with the use of synonyms); syntactic (using ambiguous word order); or semantic (confusing the meaning of words).

ANECDOTES are stories which teach a lesson, often with personal references. Not all anecdotes are humorous, but when they are told as jokes, they contain a funny twist. YARNS and TALL TALES are stories that weave a tale full of lies and exaggeration, but which are usually told as truth. They are very popular in the American humor writings about characters like Davy Crockett and Paul Bunyon, and the ability to recount a tall tale skillfully is a respected art.

The "PRACTICAL JOKE" or PRANK is simply a mischievous trick. The popularity of television shows like *Candid Camera* and *T.V.'s Bloopers and Practical Jokes* shows the acceptance and positive attitude about practical jokes in our society. Having a sense of humor about the inconveniences of these jokes is considered a virtue.

Preying on the innocence of new students or teachers sometimes serve as a kind of initiation rite. In some prep schools the carrying out of pranks is even traditional. Not all pranks carry an equal value in terms of respectability, however. Normally, the more ingenious the prank, the greater chance they have at becoming part of school legends. In early American schools, for example, when it was considered important for students at boarding schools to respond to churchbells, a typical prank incapacitated the bells so that teachers had no way to summon their students.

Pranks are also part of the initiation rites required of new members of fraternities and sororities. Hopeful initiates willingly subject themselves to all kinds of self-depricating activities in order to become members of the club. Pranksters rarely place themselves in the place of their victims. For this reason some pranks cross the line from mild derision to sadistic and dangerous jokes. Such illegal practices, referred to as HAZING, have resulted in several cases of injury or death.

SUMMARY

While there are many reasons why people laugh, language-based humor is central to the process of creating jokes. The perception of humor is possible in part because man is capable of perceiving the ambiguity of language. Much that is humorous is created by the disparity between the ideal and that which fails to imitate the ideal. It is possible to create humor by studying the conventions of a language and subverting what is expected in the listener's mind. Still, what an individual considers to be humorous on a linguistic level depends on the complex social, psychological and physical factors discussed in earlier chapters.

Language ambiguity is created as a result of the multiple levels of meaning in words. Language is both literal and figurative and devices such as homonyms, puns, oxymoron, redundancy, and incorrect grammar are all potentially humorous. Language-based humor makes use of conventions like clichés, slogans, standard metaphors, and catchwords and subverts what the listener expects. Much language-based humor involves a contrast between the colloquial and the formal, the expected and the unexpected.

CHAPTER SEVEN

THE TEACHER AS ENTERTAINER: COMIC TECHNIQUE IN THE CLASSROOM

TEACHERS have much in common with professional entertainers. Like them, teachers must hold the interest of their "audience" while they "perform." Like professional entertainers, teachers eventually learn to deal effectively with unanticipated interruptions, malfunctioning equipment, and even an occasional "heckler" in the back of the room.

Teachers who want to develop or revitalize their comic skills are in a unique position to do so because they have a (more or less) captive audience as many as five days a week. Speaking so frequently before students means that teachers can practice joke telling skills as often as they want. The purpose of this chapter is to suggest ways to help teachers learn to develop their already existing comic outlook so that it becomes an integral and consistent part of teaching.

I. LEARNING FROM PROFESSIONAL ENTERTAINERS

Good speakers like good comics are made, not born. They develop their skills over a period of time by practicing, just as a musician eventually learns to master an instrument by playing it over and over again. By practicing, you will learn what does and does not work. And the more you practice, the better you will become. In this section we will review how professional humorists develop their comic skills.

(1) STUDY POPULAR HUMOR. One of the first steps in developing a humorous style is to become more aware of the humor that surrounds you every day. Because everyone does not have the same sense of humor, much that is labeled as "humorous" may not amuse you. But it is educational to find out what is currently in vogue.

Humor is pervasive in American society. By studying published and televised humor, you will understand what others consider to be funny. There are many places to study popular humor while you practice your comic skills. When you read the comic section of your newspaper, for example, you can try to guess a humorous punchline before reading the cartoon. Or you can listen to the "one-liners" on the most popular television sit-coms.

When browsing through the humorous greeting cards in your local store, try and think of a humorous punchline before opening the card. Study humor books at your local library or listen to popular comedy albums. Once you begin collecting and dissecting the jokes that you find humorous, you will begin to better understand what makes you laugh as well as what others find humorous.

(2) **START A COMEDY LIBRARY.** If you are planning to develop your own comic style it is important to begin to THINK funny. One of the most helpful steps towards this goal is to start collecting joke books that will help you to learn how the professionals create humor. The books, albums and videotapes you collect should be ones you expect to use frequently as references or as helpful mood setters.

Your humor library should contain books on drama skills and public speaking as well as collections of jokes. Joke anthologies list thousands of witticisms and word plays. Popular joke books specialize in classroom humor or list jokes about a particular subject area. Your joke library should be a personal collection of jokes that will help you to get started as an original joke writer with humor tailored to your unique style. (A sample joke library is provided in Appendix B.)

(3) **KEEP A JOKE FILE.** Keep a list of funny things that happen in your classroom. When something humorous occurs, try to analyze why students laughed, filing incidents in categories relevant to your teaching situation. Similarly, when a joke fails, make a note of it and try to dissect what happened and how the joke might be improved in future retellings. In most cases, you should not analyze your jokes with your students as this tends to deflate the humorous mood.

Keep a record of what students laugh at among themselves, with other teachers, and when outside speakers come to visit the school. By doing this, you will discover patterns about the unique joke preferences of your students.

(4) **PLAN AHEAD.** While you are lesson planning, look at the material you will be teaching in a given week. Ask yourself when you might

want to interpolate a joke or anecdote. Some teachers feel that it is a good idea to offer a mental break by changing the subject or the approach approximately every fifteen minutes. On many of these occasions, teachers have the opportunity to use relevant jokes or anecdotes that reinforce the subject matter and make the learning experience more fun.

(5) PRACTICE YOUR JOKES. Have you ever had someone build you up for a joke only to say, "Wait a minute . . . let me get this right," and then forget the punchline? By practicing your joke, you avoid groping for words.

Teachers have little difficulty with words in daily lectures. Joke telling, however, to be most effective, must make use of specific word choices and precise word order. Joke words need to be the funniest choices of other possible alternatives.

Some professional comics recommend writing a joke first and rewriting it until the wording is as humorous as possible. When you have reached a good word choice, memorize your joke; but when you tell it, use the memorized joke only as a frame. Improvise and ad-lib as the situation allows to make the joke as personal and natural to a given situation. With practice, you can taylor the same joke to the different personalities of your student groups.

Another way to practice jokes is to tell them to a friend, spouse, or children or anyone who can help you understand what is right or wrong with it. Open yourself to criticism, however direct, about how well you tell a story or joke. Like anything else, the more you practice, the better you will become.

(6) HAVE STUDENTS SIT EVENLY ABOUT THE ROOM. Professional speakers know that they can expect a better audience reaction when people are seated together. This is true because people laugh more when they are in a group. In addition, greater rapport is established between students and the teacher when students are seated evenly about the classroom instead of being separated into little cliques whose members resist a joking relationship outside their group.

(7) USE A JOKE CUE AS A SETUP. If you have been teaching with a serious mood and disposition, students may need to be cued before you tell a joke. Otherwise, they may not understand at first that you are joking, even if the joke is very funny. This is especially true for teachers who are not accustomed to joking with students, or teachers with new students who are not yet familiar with their joking style.

A joke cue does not mean the teachers should say, "O.K., I'm about to tell a joke." Rather, it means using one of several recognizable and stylized introductions which cue people to humorous material. Something like, "Did you hear the one about . . ." or "That reminds me of a guy I knew . . ."

One form of a joke cue is to introduce a quote by a funny person. "Did you hear what Phyllis Diller said . . ." Or introduce your joke with a famous comic strip character, "Did you see Peanuts this morning?" Another type of cue is to use ridiculous names in your story. "That reminds me of my neighbor, Mr. Fumbubbler."

(8) BE BRIEF. One of the biggest mistakes speakers make when they decide to insert a joke into their speech is to talk too long. Jokes have the greatest impact when they are delivered with brevity. Rambling on with irrelevant facts will ruin even the best of jokes. In the first place, students have too much time to guess the punchline. (This is called "telegraphing.") Secondly, when you talk too long, students lose interest.

Ideally, it is best to set up your joke with a series of no more than two or three bits of information followed by a punchline. When telling a joke, sentence length should neither be too long nor too short. Pauses between phrases should be natural and the information contained in the joke should be concise enough that students are able to assimilate it quickly.

(9) TRY STANDARD JOKE FORMS. Many jokes come in recognizable standardized forms such as "knock knock jokes, "lightbulb jokes" or "elephant jokes." Standard jokes can be filed in your joke library by category. There are hundreds of stylized joke forms. Here are some sample standardized sentences you can rewrite to suit the situation:

    a. My teachers used to make me . . .
       I would get them back though, I would . . .
    b. As (my bookie) used to say . . .
       Like (my mother) used to say . . .
       Like (I) always say . . .
    c. And then there was the student who . . .
       That reminds me of (the student) who . . .
       It's like the student who . . .
    d. If you think that's funny, you should have seen . . .
    e. What is this? A . . .
    f. That reminds me of the time . . .

(10) TRY WRITING YOUR OWN MATERIAL. Mark Twain's Connecticut Yankee discovered that they were still telling the same "old" jokes when he traveled back in time to King Arthur's court. Professional joke writers explain that there is no such thing as a "new" joke; only old jokes reworked.

The best way to write your own material is to re-write someone else's joke to fit your situation. For example, instead of beginning a joke with a cue, "A funny thing happened to me on the way to the theater," substitute "school" for your destination. In other words, use the same format of an already prepared joke, but change it to make it personal and relevant.

In writing your own material, remember to consider the interests of your students over your own. Instead of telling a joke about paychecks (to students who have never had a job) or the trials of home ownership, write jokes about the things that interest your students. You can become more aware of the kind of things your students would prefer by studying the professional and published jokebooks specifically written for the age group you teach.

(11) CONSTRUCT IN-GROUP MOTIFS. Every class has its own personality. What one student group finds funny, another class will find dull. Teachers should study the personality and sense of humor of their classes before constructing in-group motifs. Class jokes should take advantage of the common experiences of the group. Having a humorous group mascot (which can be a person, place, or thing) provides a source of mirth which promotes the group cohesion.

If you are lucky enough to have a class clown, they themselves may want to serve as class mascot. You can usually rely on their sense of timing and joke telling skills, even if they need to be taught the limitations of their humorous behavior.

(12) CREATE YOUR OWN CHARACTER. Historically, comic characters have been of two primary types; the EIRON and the ALAZON. "Eirons" are witty self-deprecators. "Alazons" are boastful characters who pretend to be more than they are. Pedantic professors who pretend to know more than they do are classic alazons.

One of the more entertaining tactics teachers can use in the classroom is to take on the personality of a humorous character. In order to do this, the character must be different enough from the teacher in voice, gesture and attitude to be recognizably unique.

Teachers can cue students that they are acting out another character simply by the changing of a voice or by something more obvious like putting on a hat that tells students who that character is.

The character you build depends on your personality. Think about the type of character you would like to project; then match gestures and jokes to that character. One amusing way to enliven a lecture is to take on the voice of a historic personage.

(13) FIND A "HOOK." In the comedy business a "hook" is a recognizable phrase which always gets a laugh. Rodney Dangerfield's hook is that he doesn't get any respect. Joan Rivers asks the audience, "Can we talk?," and Jackie Gleason used to tell us "How sweet it is." The purpose of the hook is to recapture the students' attention, especially during lulls in mood.

(14) USE VARIETY. Part of what creates humor is the unexpected. With so many varieties of humorous devices from anagrams to zingers, there is no reason why teachers should tell the same kind of joke all the time. In addition, by practicing a variety of humorous devices, your joking skills will be more varied and well-rounded.

By using variety in your joke telling, you avoid having students yell out the punchline before you have a chance to get to the end of the joke.

(15) BE NATURAL. There are many ways to interpolate a joke into your lecture so that it appears to flow naturally. When telling a joke or anecdote, use the speech patterns and vocabulary you normally use. Usually, you should not make use of gestures that do not match your personality. In general, gestures should add to your words rather than detract from them.

One of the most important aspects of natural joke telling is TIMING. Deciding when to tell a joke will depend on your mood or the mood of your students at the time. To a great extent, timing is an intuitive skill. But practicing your joke delivery is the only way to improve your sense of timing.

(16) BE ASSERTIVE. When you tell your joke, project confidence. Some people reveal too many insecurities when they tell a joke, belittling themselves, belittling the joke, and stopping every few minutes to reassure themselves that the listeners have not heard the joke previously.

Tell the joke from start to finish without pausing to find out if your students are being amused by it. And if no one laughs at the punchline, don't ask them if they "got it." If they do not think the joke is funny, or if they refuse to laugh because YOU told the joke, simply shrug your shoulders and go on. After all, humor in the classroom is supposed to enhance the enjoyment of teaching, not detract from it.

(17) ENLIVEN YOUR STORIES. One of the most effective ways to enliven your humorous stories is to add dialogue. As you tell your story, change your voice to suit the character in your story. Then, animate your story by using the names of students in the classroom in the telling.

Using gestures, being animated, and walking up and down the rows keeps the students' attention on you. If you use gestures, make them natural, simple and comprehensible. A book on body language can be a helpful reference to the meaning of gestures. It is also helpful to observe public speakers on television or visitors to your school. Watch them, and practice their gestures before the mirror at home.

(18) CONTROL YOUR VOICE. The foremost voice quality for any teacher is CLARITY. If your students cannot hear what you have to say, they will more than likely begin tuning you out. And in joke telling, when students do not receive important setup data, they will not understand the punchline.

Related to clarity is the SPEED of your speech which should be natural but slow enough so that all words are articulated as separate entities. Speaking too slowly is boring and speaking too rapidly is self-defeating because students cannot assimilate your words quickly enough.

It is also important to deliver the punchline at the right speed. When you get to the punchline, slow down ever so slightly and separate it microscopically from the rest of the joke. Mastering timing requires the pause before the delivery of the punchline to be just so.

Clarity also depends on the VOLUME, loudness or power of your voice. While teachers need to project, a voice that is too loud can be irritating and a voice that is too soft is simply not heard. PITCH is the high or low tone of your voice. Pitch, like loudness, should be varied in order to avoid the dreaded monotone which propels students into ever deeper levels of slumber.

Having a pleasant, resonant voice is an important quality of dynamic speaking, humorous or otherwise. The quality of your voice conveys information about your self-confidence, leadership and poise. With a powerful voice you can increase the interest of your students so that they will be more likely to listen to the message behind your words.

(19) PERSONALIZE YOUR JOKES. Your personal experiences will always seem funnier to your students than printed versions. One way to localize your stories is by putting yourself, your family, class members or school officials into designated slots when rewriting your jokes or when creating "new" material.

(20) SPEAK AT YOUR STUDENTS' LEVEL. In general, students will be most appreciative of jokes that are moderately challenging. There is no sense telling a joke if your students cannot comprehend it because it is too difficult. And there is nothing unfunnier than having a joke that was too complex explained to you. In the same way, a joke should not be too simple as students will not find it humorous.

Puns, riddles and rhymes are usually less funny to adolescents because they are too simple. Similarly, younger children sometimes do not have the attention span to listen to anecdotes. Reviewing the humorous publications or popular television shows targeted for the age group of your students is one of the best ways to learn what they find amusing.

(21) LAUGH AT YOURSELF SOMETIMES. Some teachers are afraid that if they tell self-disparaging jokes, it may cause students to believe the teacher is incompetent in their subject area. Indeed, jokes should never be a substitute for substance. But joke telling, if anything, will improve the respect students have for you because your sense of humor reveals your humanity and teaches your students how to laugh about life.

(22) HELP STUDENTS WHO DON'T UNDERSTAND A JOKE. Being humorous in the classroom requires teachers to understand when to explain and when not to explain a punchline. It is not necessary to explain a joke just because the students do not find it amusing. It is important, however, to explain a joke when a student does not understand it. Jokes, after all, send ambiguous and often complex messages that some decipher with greater facility than others.

(23) MEMORIZE SOME "SAVE" LINES. When a joke does not succeed in creating laughter, it does not mean you still cannot create laughter. "Save lines" are expressions that anticipate a failed joke such as, "I just thought I'd throw that one in. Guess I should have thrown it out," or "No, but seriously folks . . ."

Occasionally only one student may laugh at a joke. A typical save line in this case is "I had to pay that guy five bucks to laugh" or "I don't need your pity."

II: WHAT NOT TO DO

Laughter in the classroom is supposed to have a positive influence on teaching and learning rather than a disruptive or derisive one. In this section we will discuss some of the things teachers should avoid when using humor in the classroom.

(1) DON'T MAKE FUN OF STUDENTS. Teachers should be very careful that they do not inadvertently make fun of students. Because of individual differences, teachers and students are likely to have great diversity in humor preferences. A generation or more inevitably separates us in terms of our taste in clothing, hair style, and language. Jokes that revolve around the generation gap can convey superiority and insensitivity and should be avoided.

(2) DON'T EXPLAIN A PUNCHLINE. If students do not think a joke is funny, make a note of it and move on. Students will not laugh at everything you say because their sense of humor is different. Teachers need not insult the intelligence of their students by explaining the punchline. (Of course, if the joke was too difficult, it should not have been told.) Sometimes teachers need to allow students to feel free NOT to laugh.

(3) DON'T BE NEGATIVE. Sometimes jokes are not funny because the joke teller's underlying hostility dampens the potential for mirth. Teachers should be positive when they tell jokes. Avoid being sarcastic, flippant or condescending. Teachers should never humiliate, belittle or insult students, particularly in front of their peers.

(4) DON'T FORGET TIMING. There's an old saying that the roads of Hell are paved with good intentions. If that's the case, I'm convinced there are some lesson plans down there somewhere. And there will be times when your good intention to inject a joke into your lesson does not work as you hoped it would.

Even though you have decided to tell a joke at a particular juncture in the lesson, don't forget to feel the mood of your students and try and wait until they seem receptive to a bit of humor.

The importance of timing in joke telling should not be underestimated. Timing is something you can only learn by practicing. This means that teachers must learn when to eliminate a planned joke and when to take advantage of a mood to rely on your growing repertoire of material to improvise from time to time.

(5) DON'T MAKE LIGHT OF SERIOUS ISSUES. Joking about drinking and drugs, drunk driving, sex, grades or other important issues may be interpreted as making light of these subjects. Teachers should understand the lesson behind what they say before they joke about something. In joking with students, it is important that teachers do not accidentally convey that they do not care about students, or that important issues are not important.

(6) DON'T TELL CURRENTLY POPULAR JOKES. If you happen to hear a joke on television, don't try to tell it in class the next day. If you heard it on t.v., you can rest assured that everyone else heard it too. Instead, file it away in your joke file, rewrite it to make it personal, and retell it when the perfect occasion arises.

It is often the case that popular jokes circulate around school from one student to the next. If you hear a joke at school, everyone else has probably heard it too. Anticipating this, teachers can "pull a switch" on students by rewriting a punchline. The humor comes by surprising students with an unexpected ending.

(7) DON'T USE TABOO LANGUAGE. In almost every situation that uses taboo words, the joke COULD be rewritten into a "clean" joke. "Four letter words" have a shock value that is usually inappropriate in the classroom. While obscenities may get a laugh from students, taboo words are potentially offensive. As role models, teachers should avoid the use of obscenities in the classroom.

(8) DON'T PUT YOURSELF DOWN AS A JOKE-TELLER. Before you tell a joke or story don't announce that you are not good at joke telling. If you practice your joke telling, this should not be true. But in any case, you should let the joke speak for itself without introductions. Do not tell students that a joke is "really funny" or "not that funny" before you tell it. Let them decide for themselves if the joke is funny.

(9) DON'T FORGET TO RELATE THE JOKE/STORY TO THE LESSON. Students are much more likely to accept a humorous anecdote when it is relevant to the lesson. This is exemplified in the classic situation in which a teacher, digressing to tell a funny story, is interrupted with the question, "Is this going to be on the test?"

Stories which are exclusively amusement oriented are more likely to have students packing their books for the next class rather than learning a valuable lesson you wish to enhance with a humorous story.

A teacher who is too inclined to tell jokes and stories, on a whim, frustrates students who want to learn. Even if students urge a teacher to tell more stories instead of stay with the lesson, they are likely to complain to others that the class is a waste of time.

(10) AVOID AMBIGUOUS MESSAGES. Because humorous messages are often ambiguous, it is important to understand the underlying message of a joke. One way to guarantee that students understand the right message is to explain the lesson behind the joke to students. (Don't explain the joke; just what the joke teaches.)

Students are only too quick to interpret a joke and the laughter it inspires as a teacher's insensitivity or that homework, attendance, and class itself need not be taken "seriously." Establishing a healthy laughing relationship with students has nothing to do with the importance of the subject matter. The value that teachers place on the very serious side of teaching is something that can be communicated in many ways without deleting humor from the class. Primarily, the teacher can avoid misconceptions by avoiding jokes about subjects that require serious and respectful treatment.

(11) DON'T TEACH PREJUDICE. It would seem that sexist and racist jokes are so obviously inappropriate that teachers would know to avoid them. Unfortunately, some people are not aware of their own prejudices when they joke.

The school is never a proper forum for sexist or racist humor or humor that fosters prejudice against women, ethnic minorities, religious groups, the elderly or a particular political ideology. Teachers should avoid using such jokes completely.

SUMMARY

There are a variety of effective techniques which can help teachers to develop a humorous perspective and to integrate jokes into regular curriculum. Teachers can begin a humor library, recording effective and ineffective strategies in their classrooms. For optimal results, jokes should be delivered clearly and, in some cases, dramatically, including the use of body language and dialogue. Teachers may want to use setup cues to let students know that a statement is playful. Punchlines should not be explained just because students do not find a joke humorous.

Knowing what is unacceptable humor is an important teaching skill. Teachers should not make fun of students nor should joke content ever be of the sexist or racist variety. Teachers, because of their position as role models, should be careful about bias hidden in joke content. Teachers should also avoid offensive language and ambiguous messages.

CHAPTER EIGHT

HUMOR AND TEST ANXIETY

HUMOR is most effectively used with test anxious students when students are adequately prepared for tests. Test preparation embodies not only a review of subject matter, but the teaching of study skills and test taking strategies as well.

The purpose of this chapter is to show how humor can be effectively injected into the testing environment. Humor can be a constructive teaching tool on exam review day, prior to the test itself, within the exam and during the distribution of graded exams.

I. STUDENTS

Optimally, students should be able to concentrate reasonably well while being tested, accepting small failures during the exam as surmountable and temporary. Students need to be able to sustain their motivation about completing the test which will lead them to a feeling of relief from the anxiety surrounding test taking. However, more often than not, students experience varying degrees of apprehension throughout the testing procedure which subverts the concentration necessary for optimal testscores.

Most students experience some degree of anxiety about testing. In the days leading up to a test, test anxious students may begin to lose their appetite, losing sleep as they worry about the possibilities surrounding the upcoming potential failure. Other symptoms of test anxiety include general nervousness, rapid heart beats, hot spells, a dry mouth, sweating, and butterflies in the stomach.

The following list offers some of the most common anxious thoughts about testing that students have expressed to me over the years.

   (1) No matter how much I study, I don't feel like I'm ever ready.

   (2) I feel like I'm going to forget everything I studied.

(3) I just blank out.

(4) I start not caring a few days before the test.

(5) I panic about not making it to the exam on time. I almost always arrive late. Then I can't stop worrying that time will run out.

(6) I get depressed. I start thinking, "what's the use of trying?"

(7) I get worried that I didn't study the right material.

(8) I just want to get the test over with. Sometimes I even turn it in without going back over my answers just to be done with it.

There are many factors which lead to test anxiety. Most often, the student views the test as a measure of their overall intelligence and the fear of failing is overwhelming. Some students have a great fear of failing because they have failed a great deal in the past and they are fearful about failing again. Failing, test anxious students tell themselves, will disappoint parents or embarrass them when they see that other students are able to pass.

The fear of failing a test of intelligence is part of most testing situations. From the very beginning of the school years, students understand that their aptitude is going to be compared to the abilities of other group members and the pressure of competition can become more important to an individual than it should. It is most destructive when the student allows self-defeating thoughts to cloud their minds so thoroughly, that the concentration necessary for studying and optimal test taking is diminished.

It is for this reason that humor is so important to the testing procedure because laughter can act as a tension-reducing mechanism. Humor has the potential to help test anxious students to relieve some of the negative tension before an exam. But the integration of humor into the testing procedure does not confront the main cause of test anxiety—the poorly prepared student.

II. TEACHERS

Because inadequate preparation is one of the main causes of test anxiety, one of the main tactics in the reduction of destructive tension is to help students to prepare for their exams. Students usually feel less anxious if they feel that the teacher has adequately covered the subject in class.

Helping students prepare for exams goes beyond reviewing subject matter. Some, if not all students need to learn study skills which include memorization exercises, how to prepare a good study environment at home, how to study consistently as opposed to "cramming," and so on.

This kind of encouragement and coaching needs to be an ongoing process because there are few students who are self-motivated enough that they can do without the teacher's persistent concern, especially in subject areas for which students have little interest.

When teachers create an environment in which testing is central, learning becomes secondary. In such an environment, test anxiety is likely to be high with questions from students pertaining less to comprehension of the subject matter and more to the likelihood of inclusion of any given piece of information on the test. As exam day approaches, students are more likely to seek cues from the teacher about the test content and emphasis. Humorous and serious remarks alike are interpreted merely as hints to be deciphered about what is going to be on the test.

One of the ways teachers can avoid the over-emphasis on grades in the classroom is to help students understand that the measure of the aptitude and worth comes from behavior and talents unrelated to their test grades. Providing (graded) *creative* projects which allow students to reveal other levels of their talents will help them to see that written test grades are just one form of the measurement of their worth.

III. THE TEST

(1) **REVIEWING FOR THE EXAM.** Of the many sources of anxiety surrounding exams, one of the most common causes of preoccupation concerns the form and content of the exam. Students want to know how many pages to expect, what kinds of questions will be asked, and how long they will be allowed to test. They want to know if the questions will be essay, multiple choice or true and false and what specifically will be included on the exam and what will not.

The exam review is particularly important for the test-anxious student since they are more likely to be worried about the unfamiliarity of the test situation. By going over test directions the day before the exam, test-anxious students can know what is expected of them. This also saves the teacher from Murphy's First Law of Test-Giving: No matter how clearly directions are worded on the exam, someone will not understand them. In addition, by assuring that everyone understands what to do on exam day, the teacher and students avoid using time going over directions and wasting valuable test time.

Since the anxiety level on review day is considerably lower than it will be on the test day, test review day offers a good opportunity for teachers to make use of humor to relieve anxiety. Students are more likely to feel playful on a non-test day and joking can set up the less anxious testing atmosphere. On test review day, teachers can humorously express understanding about the student's plight to lower anxiety. At the same time, joking should not cue students that the use of humor is making light of the exam or the serious expectations of requirements on their test performance.

Students want to know what is expected of them on the exam, especially if they have never tested with an instructor before. It is important to assure students that an exam is fair and that content is indicative of material covered in the course and text. Students should know that if they study, they have a better chance of doing well.

Test taking advice that teachers give on a test review day depends on the age and education level of the students. The following general tips are helpful at any level.

(1) Study a little every day rather than cramming the night before an exam.

(2) Do not change daily routines on test days.

(3) Do not change the diet before a test. Not eating or eating too much may cause students to feel drousy during the exam.

(4) To relax, try some deep breathing exercises. These can be done before or during the exam. Exercise also helps relieve tension.

(5) Get a good night's sleep the night before the exam.

(6) On exam day arrive a bit early. Avoid talking to other students about what they studied or what they "heard" about the exam.

(7) Wear comfortable clothes during the exam. Some researchers believe that students test better when they dress well for an exam.

(8) Take care of biological needs before the exam. Use the restroom and get a drink of water before the test.

(9) Bring extra pens and pencils to the exam in case the lead breaks or the pen runs out of ink.

Test anxious students usually appreciate a test review which includes hints on how to take exams. Here are a few samples of advice to help students understand how to take tests.

(1) Students should not spend too much time when they forget an answer. Try marking the item and return to it at the end of the test.

(2) Do not leave items blank on a test. At least attempt to answer every question.

(3) When students do not know an answer, they can use the process of elimination to make an "educated guess" as opposed to choosing an answer randomly.

(4) Review the entire test before beginning. Pace time based on the point value of each section.

(5) Allow time at the end of the test to review answers for "silly errors."

(6) Avoid changing answers during the test review unless the second guess is a sure answer.

Giving students helpful advice about how to take tests makes the students feel they have more power over the test situation. Feeling powerless is one of the causes of test anxiety.

(2) THE TESTING ENVIRONMENT. Students feel particularly anxious about the unexpected on exam day. Changing classrooms or seating plans, being tested on unexpected material, changing the expected format and especially the dreaded "pop quiz," are all great anxiety provokers. On the other hand, such tactics are often necessary because students who are not expected to be test ready at all times may begin to relax until exam time.

It is important, though not always possible, for the teacher to provide the optimal testing conditions during an exam. Cheating is often a crime of opportunity rather than a premeditated act and, if possible, should be avoided. For the test-anxious student, there is nothing more disconcerting than to have the opportunity to see other students doing something different on an exam. Optimally, students should have as much room as possible. They should be spaced far enough apart that they are not tempted to look at other papers and so that no one can disturb them by trying to see their exams.

During the test, teachers should strive to avoid interruptions as much as possible. It is bothersome for students and teachers to have their test interrupted with announcements or fire drills that waste valuable time. Similarly, visitors who come into the room whispering loudly, disturb the concentration of testing students.

Interruptions during tests cannot always be avoided, but they can be anticipated. When the teacher deals fairly with an interruption (allowing more time, for example), students feel less anxious about the effect that disruptions will have on their exam grades.

(3) TIME CONSTRAINTS. Another source of test anxiety is the time limitations of the testing situation. Some students become so preoccupied about time that they can hardly concentrate, wasting valuable minutes that should be devoted to answering questions. Teachers can help to alleviate time anxiety by preparing exams which can be completed realistically in the time alloted. When a student has a severe problem with time anxiety, the teacher or school counselor may be able to work with that particular problem on an individual basis. Test taking students are usually quite adamant about fair rules in test taking, particularly as regards giving extra time to individual students.

Understanding the constraints of time and being able to sense the passing of time is one of the test taking skills that students eventually learn. While students must realize that time is limited and that it is passing, awareness of time during the test should be as unobtrusive as possible. Writing the remaining time on the chalkboard can interrupt a student's concentration as well as heightening anxiety. Quiet but clearly visible clocks can be effective while causing less noise and interruption.

(4) PRE-TEST JOKING. Moments prior to the beginning of an exam, feelings about the test have usually peaked. Most people would agree that a joke told before an exam can release some of this energy. Teachers must be careful, however, to tell a joke which is harmless. Offending students right before an exam is more distracting than helpful.

As we have seen thoughout this text, the sense of humor in any given class is as diverse as the individuals who make up the group. In addition to differences in the levels of seriousness, there are sexual, ethnic and religious differences which differentiate members of the class. In joking about a student's sex, race, age or religion, teachers forfeit the healthy potential a pre-test joke should have; to release pent-up feelings about the test.

Pre-test jokes should be brief and told while distributing exams. This is important because students do not want their test time wasted for any reason.

(5) THE TEST. There are varying points of view regarding the ordering of test items on the exam. Most test experts have promoted the idea that presenting easier items at the beginning of the exam eases the student into the test during the initial high-anxiety moments of the test. Others have offered that easy initial items lower student expectations so that they are not prepared for difficult material later in the exam. Finally, there are those who believe that it is preferable to offer a random placement of easy and difficult items.

The disagreement on this point is a reflection of the different way that individuals react to exams. By advising students to spend the first two or three minutes studying the exam, students can decide for themselves how they would like to proceed on the test.

Periodically, on the test itself, teachers can inject humorous items as appropriate. While some researchers assert that humorous items may be distracting, a small amount of humor of the harmless variety should not cause students to lose concentration and may help relieve some of their anxiety during the test.

(6) RETURNING EXAMS. There are many tactics which are sure to increase anxiety during the distribution of graded exams. After all, grades were the cause of everyone's anxiety in the first place. Since it has been shown that past failure effects anxiety, the distribution of graded exams is as important as any other activity surrounding the testing process.

I have always been amazed by Hollywood stereotypes of teachers returning exams while sadistically humiliating students with hypobolic insults. Hollywood teachers are often portrayed as being frustrated about the mediocrity of their students' compositions and believing that only doses of humiliation will snap them back into shape. Said one sarcastic Hollywood teacher, "Next time try writing in your mother tongue, Mr. Jones. I assume that is English." In the real classroom situation, I can hardly imagine such a tactic as being effective.

Similarly, while going over exams I have known teachers who could not resist sharing some of the most ridiculous answers with the rest of the class. But announcing a student's ignorance to the class gets a laugh at the expense of the slow or ill-prepared student. Instead of public ridicule, encouraging remarks can be made on the exams of the failing students with an invitation to come in and talk in private about the test.

Announcing that exams are being passed out from high to low grades or vice versa targets the slow student. Making public comments about individual grades is embarrassing to most students. There is probably nothing quite so humiliating as being laughed at by a class of students, the victim of a teacher's joke while distributing exams.

Folding exams so grades can be viewed privately, and distributing them in random order or alphabetically, can ease the anxiety caused by peer pressure. Handing back exams can be a time to alleviate anxiety about the present and future exams. As on test day, an initial joke can relieve the greatest amount of tension.

SUMMARY

Humor can be an effective teaching tool which relieves test anxiety on the test review day, just prior to the exam, on the exam itself, and during the distribution of exams. The best way to relieve test anxiety is to prepare students adequately for their tests. Exams should be administered in the optimal environment. Tests should be fair and indicative of course content. All of these factors help students be more receptive to humor in the classroom in general and around the testing situation in particular.

CHAPTER NINE

CLASS CLOWNS AND OTHER JOYS
OF TEACHING

"Let's be thankful for the fools. If it weren't for them, the rest of us could not succeed."

MARK TWAIN

I. THE SOCIAL FUNCTION OF THE FOOL

WHILE CLOWNS have traditionally occupied a low and ridiculed position in society, their role has nevertheless been an extremely important one. Whether they played the fool in a primitive island tribe, or as a wandering minstrel or comic stock character in a traveling theater company, or even as court jester in the castle of kings, their existence and function has been a consistent one. It was the fool, the clown, the buffoon and the comedian who specialized in a humorous perspective of life, even in the wake of the hardships and the drudgery of life. And it was the fool who expressed the deepest thoughts and fears of the group, causing laughter to release potentially hostile or anxious tension.

Some fools were appreciated for their humorous wit while others were mischievous pranksters. Still others were considered humorous for their physical deformities or mental deficiencies. Dwarfs, midgets and hunchbacks often played the role of the fool both at court and in early theater. Circus clowns still use make-up and costumes to exaggerate deformities and to make themselves appear physically ridiculous by wearing flipper like shoes, bald spots, big lips, large posteriors or red noses.

93

Just as clowns have always served the wider social community, class clowns served the mini-society of the classroom. Even Socrates was said to have endured some clowning from his student Plato who supposedly made fun of his teacher by paroding his stories. About Socrates' famous allegory in which the ugly duckling metamorphosized into a swan, Plato is said to have retold the story joking that he himself had metamorphosized into a crow which pecked the bald spot on his teacher's head.

Learning conditions of early schools provided fertile ground for class clowning. Under the constant supervision of the headmaster, circumstances were unpleasant at best. Students had to endure the heat or cold of the room; Chairs consisted of hard benches shared by many other students; and studying one's Latin or math lessons was a grueling task that went on for hours on end. Surely the prankster provided a much appreciated diversion from such conditions.

The modern classroom environment hardly equals the unpleasant learning conditions of yesteryear. Not only has modern technology allowed for greater physical comforts in the classroom, but developments in discipline suggest more humane treatment of students and reforms in curriculum and teaching methodology have made learning less excruciating.

Class clowns often provide the release of tension so conducive to a positive learning environment. The rigors of learning, while not as severe as they once were, still require periods of relaxation in order to facilitate high levels of interest and concentration on the part of students. Class clowns can provide the joking that causes the class to experience group laughter which promotes group cohesion and togetherness. And sometimes, this laughter is the only socially acceptable way that students may express feelings about the constrained environment of the classroom.

II. PROFILE OF THE CLASS CLOWN

To a certain extent, most people have a bit of a clown in them. In most cases, people choose to repress exhibitionistic and non-conformist behavior when they become members of a group, especially in school and church where obedience is expected. Yet it is precisely when laughter is forbidden that clowns function best.

There is no one reason why some students are more inclined to become class clowns than others. Sometimes, their clowning behavior has been positively reinforced over many years so that joking is a skill they have cultivated and developed. Some students turn to humor as a socially acceptable way to resist authority as a part of the maturation process. Others may be hiding many types of fears and insecurities behind a barage of jokes. For students who cannot gain popularity by means of their good looks or athletic prowess, acting as the class clown can be a way of being liked and accepted by fellow students. But understanding the individual causes and motivations behind the behavior of clowns does not lessen the fact that clowning is disconcerting when it is disruptive.

The class clown's approach and outlook are as varied as are their personalities. They may be wits, noisemakers or jokers. Some are optimists, others pessimists, and still others are somewhere in between. Some are great punsters, others excel at one liners.

The following class clown profiles represent stereotypical overviews. In reality, class clowns are difficult to describe because their personalities are as unique as the personality of any individual student. Nevertheless, these generalizations hold a certain degree of truth and will be helpful for understanding how to better deal with class clowns.

(1) THE SELF-DEPRECATOR. The self-deprecating clown is a student who allows us to laugh at them by ridiculing their mental or physical flaws. They are usually well-liked by their classmates, though not necessarily feared or respected. Essentially we laugh at them instead of laughing at ourselves.

Many professional comics are, in fact, self-deprecators. Rodney Dangerfield tells us he "don't get no respect;" Woody Allen is the only guy in the office who can't get a date with the office whore; Joan Rivers laments the size of her breasts telling jokes about how small they are as well as jokes about how ugly she is; Phyllis Diller is such a bad cook she admits that her family gave her a stove that flushes; and Steve Martin tells us he's a jerk in his film by that title.

(2) THE HOSTILE WIT. The hostile wit is often an anti-social clown who is antagonistic to rules that make demands upon his behavior. Hostile wits utilize hostile humor such as sarcasm against the teacher or fellow students or generally "make fun" at the expense of others. They may be feared by classmates who view them as powerful, influential and threatening.

What makes the hostile wit distinctive is the outward targeting of other people with critical humor. His jokes are often accompanied by profanity, making defiant use of forbidden language.

One form of hostile humor includes throwing objects at other students or at the teacher. This type of clowning may produce uncomfortable laughter amongst the students who are unsure how the teacher will react to this challenge of authority. Another form of hostile humor is to verbally ridicule other students after they have answered a question.

Typically, victims of hostile clown humor never point out the real culprits because they are too afraid of them. Thus the embarrassed victims of whoopee cushions, braid pulling, pencil jabbing, book spilling and so on, are not likely to antagonize their tormentor by telling the teacher what has really happened. Part of the fun for the hostile clown is seeing the wrong person punished for a crime.

Hostile wits, willing to make jokes at the expense of others, are usually not good about "taking a joke" themselves. In fact, their constant attempts to insure that the class concentrates its laughter on others is a symptom of their own fear of being laughed at. Once the humorous attention is focused on them, they often become hostile or aggressive.

Hostile wits generally have a negative attitude towards school and classroom tasks. This may be manifested in a good deal of absenteeism and their lack of good preparation for classroom tasks. Hostile clowns sometimes use frustrating tactics with which to challenge teachers. These include forgetting about exams, claiming they are unable to answer questions about assignments during class, or answering incorrectly and sarcastically.

(3) THE MIRTH-MAKER/SOCIAL COMMENTATOR. Mirth makers just like to "goof around." Their humor consists of innocent commentary or light-hearted teasing which primarily has an entertainment value. Behind their silliness is no great hidden intention. Their jokes are harmless and their sense of humor is manifested in easy and frequent laughter.

Mirth-makers can and often do have a positive effect on the class, but only if their behavior is somewhat controlled. Teachers can call upon them when joking is appropriate and these students are usually guaranteed to come up with something witty. Mirth-makers can be a great boon to the classroom, lending personality, increasing morale, and helping students cope with the task of learning and growing up.

The mirth-maker sometimes acts as social commentator for the rest of the class. In this role, their humor is not directed at their inadequacies, like the self-deprecator, nor do they attack others with their jokes like the hostile clown. Rather, they are able to see the humor and irony in which the entire class can identify and help the class to share in a common experience of laughter.

There are several general payoffs which clowns can hope to expect with their humorous behavior. Most importantly, their clowning is a bid for CONTROL and ATTENTION of the class. In addition their jokes provide themselves and others a diversion from boredom. Finally, clowning can be a creative outlet which offers a challenging use of their intelligence.

Playing the part of the class clown brings forth a variety of feelings for the comic. Undoubtedly, the approval of fellow classmates in the form of laughter produces a certain ELATION. Yet the excitement of being the center of attention may be accompanied by a sense of being made the fool. Likewise, the role of class clown may carry with it a degree of pressure in the sense that the class clown is often called upon to perform on-the-spot.

Even though being a class clown usually is not condoned by parents or school officials, this disapproval and accompanying punishment is usually not a deterrent. By the time a student has earned the reputation of "class clown," it is a difficult role to shun, even if they want to. Peers begin to expect certain behavior and often goad the jokster on to more daring stunts.

III. DISCIPLINING THE CLASS CLOWN

(1) **HISTORICAL OVERVIEW.** When teachers ask students to conform to group rules, they are limiting student expression by asking them to control their spontaneity and creativity. Under normal classroom circumstances, group goals take priority over individual preferences and group members are required to conform to the group's code of behavior. Orderly behavior is desirable because it makes group activities possible and profitable for the greatest number of students. While conformity is not always optimal, it is usually necessary. It is also the breeding ground for comic dissent and class clowndom.

Early educators were deeply concerned with compliance to the classroom code of behavior. Students were expected to be silent around adults and respectful at all times. Deviants in class were soon punished into submission. Typical clowning included telling lies (to get someone else in trouble), namecalling, swearing, or, as some early diaries describe it, "hooping and hollering."

Class clowning was almost always punished publicly. Not only did the clown have to endure the pain of his or her punishment, but it was usually accompanied by derisive laughter as well. This supposedly allowed the rest of the class to learn never to repeat the crime.

One of the most common humiliations inflicted upon the class clown was to force them to sit on a wooden jackass or to hang a wooden ass around their necks. Another popular punishment required them to stand in a corner for long periods of time while wearing the donkey or dunce cap.

In some cases special punishments were devised such as making a boy sit with the girls or with the younger students. Class clowning might also result in much more severe consequences like disgrace, suspension or expulsion. Nevertheless, despite the potentially severe consequences, it appears that there have always been a few students who were willing to take a chance in order to engage in some clowning behavior as a diversion from the rigors of learning.

(2) TEACHER ATTITUDES TOWARDS CLOWNING. Class clowning, like clowning in the wider society, is a behavior that is essentially rebellious and challenging. For this reason, teachers generally view class clowns as a negative element in the classroom. Most often, clowns are seen as unruly attention seekers and disruptive troublemakers. Sometimes class clowns are unwanted because teachers feel that they rob learning time with entertainment. Nevertheless, the positive social function of the class clown cannot be underestimated.

Because class clowns can be astute observers of classroom events, some teachers feel threatened by a student's attempt to undermine or expose their weaknesses. The teacher who is insecure or afraid in the classroom may feel threatened by the class clown and instinctively respond to clowning with rebuke and punishment.

The teacher's attitude about class clowning can establish codes of behavior about laughter in the classroom in general. While it is important to control the use of diversion and entertainment in the classroom, putting down every attempt at clowning can discourage the expression of laughter at all.

By allowing some clowning in the classroom, teachers can show that they have a sense of humor as long as that humor is in good taste and expressed at appropriate times. By doing this, teachers teach respect, both for authority and for fellow students. Teachers can serve as role models to show that they can laugh at themselves or that people can laugh at one another, but that it should be done with all due respect and good nature. The lesson taught with healthy humor teaches students courtesy and respect, cooperation and tolerance.

(3) DISCIPLINING THE CLASS CLOWN. Over the years the issue of discipline in the classroom has been hotly debated by teachers and parents alike. Views on discipline range from advocates of harsh discipline to those who do not believe any discipline is needed at all. The solution is probably somewhere in between. Teachers are charged with the difficult task of determining what communities, parents and principals want, while doing what is best for the group. This includes treating students as individuals with unique and individual needs.

Very simply, the problem with disciplining the class clown is that parents, teachers and students do not all agree on what is best. Some teachers categorize all clowns as hostile wits, using hostile put-downs to stop the clowning. Unfortunately, this kind of confrontation often only succeeds in creating more hostile clowning.

Hostile put-downs are not for every clown or every situation and teachers need to understand their students before using such tactics. Class clowns who are self-deprecators, for example, may be indicating that they experience feelings of inadequacy that would only be aggravated with teacher put-downs. In general, teachers should strive to minimize deprecating behavior in the classroom whether self or other directed. Harmful humor which causes derisive laughter should be controlled whenever possible.

Sometimes the self-deprecator is a slow learner who makes fun of themselves rather than admitting they do not understand something. Making a special effort to allow them to participate in class discussions on easier items will reduce opportunities for them to cause a disruption during class.

Similarly, meeting hostile clowning with hostile put-downs is likely to create even more confrontation. Hostile class clowns may need professional help. Some come from homes that are so intolerable, that the classroom is their only forum of expression. Sometimes a counselor can help. But in dealing with the hostile class clown, it becomes especially important that they be sensitized to the feelings of their victims.

Some teachers prefer not to acknowledge the class clown, believing that if they are ignored, they will eventually stop their clowning. However, when the teacher does nothing, they imply that "anything goes." When teachers ignore the misbehavior of the class clown, other students learn that there is no retribution for undesirable behavior. Teachers will find that permissiveness is no way to discipline and ignoring a class clown will not make them go away. Harsh and unloving discipline often causes resentment and more unwanted behavior.

Essentially, the best way to deal with class clowning is to create a classroom environment which does not encourage disruptive behavior. Not all class clowning needs to be discouraged. The healthy humor of the mirth-maker and social commentator should be encouraged. However, when clowning becomes disruptive, the best interests of the group are disturbed, and this kind of clowning is to be avoided. The following general guidelines should serve to avoid classroom conditions that encourage disruptive clowning:

1. Be flexible about group rules against individual needs.
2. Avoid double standards of punishment which are based on sex, race or religion.
3. Be sensitive to changes in class mood.
4. Gear lessons to all intellectual levels which must sometimes share the same classroom.
5. Smile and show enthusiasm; assure students that you like them, and that you like what you do.
6. Be courteous and respectful of students.
7. Be consistent and fair.
8. Never forget your role as teacher and adult; avoid trying to be "pals" with students.
9. Encourage students often; avoid ridicule.
10. Avoid excessive punishments; beware of public punishment and humiliation that may only cause greater conflict.
11. Make sure students understand the law; allow students to opinionate about the logic and fairness of class rules and be open to negotiation in some cases.
12. Come to school well rested and prepared with lessons that are interesting.

Class clowns can and often do have a positive effect on the class but only if their behavior is somewhat controlled. Teachers can call upon them when joking is appropriate and these students are usually guaranteed to come up with something witty when asked.

Teachers can take advantage of the need on the part of the class clown for attention and recognition by teaching them how to use appropriate classroom humor which is integrated at the right moments. Just as disruptive humor should be discouraged, healthy humor should be encouraged and cultivated. The only discipline or special attention required for classroom mirth-makers is that they understand timing and know that a good joke has its time and place.

(4) A SPECIAL NOTE TO SUBSTITUTE TEACHERS. Remember the elation your class experienced when you found out there would be a sub? Not only did it mean a day off from the usual routine, but also a relaxation of the strict discipline. Substitute teachers are particularly vulnerable to class clowning primarily because they are unfamiliar with the group's chemistry and hierarchy. Here are a few hints especially for substitute teachers:

1. Avoid excessive discipline as an attempt to overcompensate for student disrespect.
2. Try a humorous perspective to avoid frustration about student challenges.
3. Get advice about your classes from permanent teachers.
4. Observe students in the halls and lunchroom to get to know them better.
5. Do not announce to classes that you are "new" or that you do not know what to do. Take control.
6. Be natural and flexible; honest, straightforward and positive.
7. In case teachers have no lessons planned, come to class prepared with lessons or games challenging to the level of the class.
8. Try and bring a breath of fresh air to students.
9. Read a book on substitute teaching to get more ideas on how to improve the substitute experience.

SUMMARY

Conditions in any constrained environment such as the classroom promote the rebellious expression of class clowns. In some cases, clowning has a morale-building influence on the group, while other kinds of clowning are negative or disruptive. These include self-deprecating humor which invites derisive laughter and hostile clowning.

Disciplining the class clown calls for situational ethics that depends on the relationship between communities, school leaders, parents, teachers, the clowning student and the rest of the class. The role of the teacher in dealing with the class clown is crucial because a teacher's attitude towards the class clown can influence the limitations on laughter in the group in general.

SUGGESTED READING

Barbara Pronin: Substitute Teaching: A Handbook for Hassle-Free Subbing. New York, St. Martin's Press, 1983.

Wegmann, Robert G.: Classroom Discipline: A Negotiable Item. Today's Education, LXV, 3: 92-93, 1976. Reprinted in part as Tips on Discipline. Today's Education, LXXI, 44-45, 1982.

CHAPTER TEN

HUMOR AND CREATIVE DRAMA
IN THE CLASSROOM

THE IDEA OF integrating drama into the curriculum is not a new one. Most educators would agree that the dramatic curriculum is dynamic and energetic, but thus far, more traditional and sedate methodologies prevail. In this chapter we will discuss the dramatic curriculum and how humor can be used in a dramatic context to promote both the enjoyment of learning and the retention of subject matter.

I. THE DARTMOUTH METHOD

The Dartmouth Method of foreign language learning was developed at Dartmouth College during the 1960s. While foreign language enrollment was dropping at other colleges around the nation, enrollment at Dartmouth was increasing at a phenomenal rate. This was due, for the most part, to the dramatic methodologies of John Rassias, professor of romance languages and literature.

The Dartmouth method was originally developed in 1965 as an intensive course for Peace Corps volunteers. The method consists of a "total immersion" into the foreign language which occurs in Rassias's classes from the moment the bell rings on the first day of class. Classes are supplemented with tutorial drill sessions which reinforce the master class. For the many students who tend to neglect their foreign language studies during their regular homework time, these sessions function as essential supplements.

Professor Rassias was a student of drama in Paris before dedicating his life to the teaching of foreign languages. In the Dartmouth method, Rassias completely integrates drama and humor into his teaching. According to one writer (*Time Magazine,* August 16, 1976), John Rassias is described as having "about as many routines as Henny Youngman." In his most dramatic moments Rassias has expressed himself by throwing chairs out of classroom windows, though his protégés tend to be more conservative.

The Dartmouth method is quite adaptable and is now used at over 60 universities across the country, all reporting success with the program. While one of the program's main attractions is its vitality, the reason for its success has more to do with the fact that students in Dartmouth classes retain information better than students who study under less exciting models. Some attribute the success of the Dartmouth foreign language program to the emotional experience linked to the study of facts. Others would attribute its success to the repetition used in the drills and master class.

The Dartmouth method can teach us a great deal about the value of a dynamic curriculum. Excitement and drama attract students in the same way that it attracts all people. Classes that are dull and boring, whatever the subject, cause students to reject education altogether. The high dropout rate in high schools and colleges is due, in part, to the boredom of stagnant classrooms.

II. SIMULATION LEARNING

"Simulation" is the act of imitating. The possibilities for simulation experiences in the classroom are limitless and can be adapted to any subject. In order to create a simulation experience, teachers convince their students that they are in another time or place other than the classroom. Students learn by living the roles of characters in a fantasy drama. Courtroom simulations can be used to teach justice (or injustice); transporting students to a Civil War confrontation can teach them history; allowing them to take on the role of political figures can help them to understand the complexities of leadership and responsibility.

Students love a simulation experience because it makes the learning of facts feel important. When history becomes personal, students tend to care more about it. In addition, simulation dramas are usually social experiences in which everyone in the class participates. Such methods contribute to the group's sense of togetherness and belonging.

Simulation drama requires no extra funds for textbooks or supplies. Teachers and students in a simulation experience are only limited by their imaginations. In some cases, several classes can participate in the drama so that the simulation project becomes a school affair.

Part of the fun of simulation experiences is the excitement of antici-pation (for students and teachers). Students want to come to class to find out what is going to happen next. Teachers allow students to discover subject matter as the drama unfolds.

A simulation experiment used in a Fort Lauderdale junior high school will serve as an example of one possibility. In this case, a Spanish teacher arranged to have a friend come to her classroom to steal her purse in front of the students. The students were unaware at first that the drama had begun. Eventually, the class learned the rules of the dra-matic game (in Spanish) and realized that they would play the role of de-tectives who would solve the mystery of the missing pocketbook. As the drama progressed over the weeks, the offender was caught and brought to trial. In this case the teacher herself was surprised when her own stu-dents brought her to the stand and accused her of hiring the man to steal her purse for the insurance money.

III. CREATIVE DRAMA IN THE CLASSROOM

There are multiple opportunities for creative drama in the class-room. PANTOMIME exercises allow students to practice body lan-guage and to understand their physical expressions. In addition, allowing students to move their bodies is good exercise for young people with extra energy. Pantomime exercises can be done alone or with other students to teach cooperation, trust, and coordination. Eventually, when dialogue is added to pantomime, students learn to be more effective communicators.

Creative drama in the classroom is a perfect vehicle for artistic ex-pression as well. Talking PUPPETS, MASKS and other ARTWORK can be integrated into the regular curriculum as vehicles for storytelling or lecturing about almost any subject. In many ways, this kind of artistic creativity allows students who do not perform well on standard tests and oral drills to have a successful experience.

Finally, creative drama can involve students in the creation of origi-nal works. The teaching of IMPROVISATION, for example, allows students (accustomed to being non-participating television viewers) to use their imaginations in order to create their own dramas. Improvised skits performed for the rest of the class are educational in that the stu-dents learn performing skills that will help them to function in front of other people.

IV: THE IMPORTANCE OF TIMING: WHEN TO USE HUMOR

Humor, whether it is in a dramatic or non-dramatic context, should be integrated into teaching when teachers feel that the time is right for a joke. Knowing when to use humor is a skill that combines experience and intuition with a thorough knowledge of your students. Here are a few ideas about when to inject humor into your teaching.

(1) **START CLASS WITH A JOKE.** When students come into the classroom they are full of energy and expectation. Joke telling is one way to help them release some of that energy.

Jokes that start your class do not necessarily have to be related to the lesson of the day. However, humor should relate to some issue of student concern such as current events, school functions or an uncoming sport's event.

One "intro" I have used with university students on the first day of class is to list my qualifications in a fun way. I tell students, "Some of you may have heard about me already. My former students have called me 'unfair, intolerable, and infinitely boring.' But enough of their compliments . . ." This joke is intended to release tensions caused by fears that university students have about the competence and humanity of their professors.

Humor is an effective means of calling attention which allows students to release that extra energy and to come together as a group with the mutual experience of laughter.

(2) **USE HUMOR TO GET TO KNOW STUDENTS' NAMES.** Max Eastman tells the story of a professor at the University of Göttingen in the sixteenth century:

> Wishing to enroll a student named Warr in his class, he asked him his age, and upon receiving the reply that the student was thirty years of age, he exclaimed; 'Aha!, so I have the honor of seeing the Thirty Year's War!'

Having to memorize student's names is a real job at the beginning of a school term, requiring teachers to learn as many as 90-100 names in the course of three to four days. But learning names can be a great source of fun for the class.

One way teachers learn names is to put name tags on everyone's shirt, or nametags on the desks. This is a serious and effective approach. It is more fun, however, to play memory games with students. One memory game requires you to remember a student's name by some association about their physical feature or dress. Remembering that "Ruth" has red hair can help remind you that her name begins with an "r." This memory game can help students learn how to study anything that must be memorized.

(3) USE HUMOR TO TEACH STUDY AIDS. Humor can be used to teach students how to improve their memory and concentration skills. Vocabulary drills, spelling bees and other language games are fun ways to amuse students while they are learning. Acronyms, crossword puzzles, and dictionary exercises can be structured as games which promote healthy competition among students.

Joke telling requires students to memorize, to practice concise deliveries, and to improvise and ad-lib. In addition, joke telling teaches natural and positive communications skills that can be used in a practical way as students increase their social roles outside the classroom. By allowing, even requiring, students to develop joke telling skills, teachers provide a forum wherein students can see how others react to their jokes and how they can improve their humorous skills.

(4) TEACH HUMOR TECHNIQUES TO STUDENTS. Most people discover that humor can be an effective tool in all facets of job relations. Yet rarely do teachers, outside special courses in public speaking, instruct students how to be funny. Instead, the development of humor skills is left up to the individual. This should not be true. More attention should be placed on teaching our students how to create humor since it is such an important skill in job and personal relations.

Teachers who require oral presentations of students, for example, might show students how to start their speeches with a joke, how to sprinkle their oral presentations with humor, and how to leave an oral presentation with a humorous punchline. Too many teachers allow students to stand motionless before their peers, mechanically reading dull reports in muffled monotones so that they have poor delivery skills even after years of oral reports.

Teaching humor to students may involve teaching them to have a sense of humor. This is important, especially when a student perceives a minor event to have greater significance than it should. As a role model, the teacher is in a good position to instruct students who do not laugh that laughing at themselves and the underside of life is one way to cope with adversity.

(5) DESIGN HUMOROUS BULLETIN BOARDS. The display of humor on bulletin boards is a visual way to show students that humor is allowed and promoted in the classroom. Any humorous device can be utilized to teach lessons with bulletin boards. Comic strips, cartoons and other visual jokes invite a humorous atmosphere. The use of language-based humor is a valuable way to reinforce vocabulary or other lessons.

(6) **USE HUMOR TO CHANGE THE SUBJECT.** At some point during the class, teachers need to move from one activity to the next. Telling a joke at a pivotal point is a great way to let students stretch. Laughter after a good joke is often accompanied by movements like shifting in seats or stretching. This change-of-subject joke does not need to be related to the material at hand as long as it effectively changes the class mood.

Students probably need to relax and shift about every fifteen minutes, although this depends on age and interest in the subject matter. A joke integrated into the regular lecture is a perfect opportunity to let students keep their concentration strong.

A joke that changes the subject is also effective in waking your sleeping students. Students who have stopped listening will begin to wonder what everyone is laughing about and pay better attention.

(7) **USE HUMOR IN QUESTION ANSWER SESSIONS.** Question and answer sessions are important because they provide a time when students reveal what they do and do not understand about a particular lesson. There is no such thing as a bad question, but questions are sometimes humorous for the same reason that anything is funny; something appears to be incongruous with the situation or offers an unusual or surprising association. Answers can be just as funny, because the speech that takes place during such sessions is unrehearsed and subject to slips of the tongue and occasional witticisms.

Question and answer periods do not have to be tedious. It is up to the teacher to create a relaxed and friendly mood that invites some verbal repartee. Students love to challenge teachers and humor is a socially acceptable vehicle for healthy confrontations. However, the teacher is always the arbitor of fairness in the classroom and at the same time may need to control the humor so that it is positive in nature rather than derisive or disruptive.

(8) **ENHANCE YOUR SUBJECT MATTER WITH JOKES.** Whatever you teach, there are plenty of jokes about your subject that you can begin collecting. There is something funny about everything, even math and the sciences which are generally considered to be relatively dry and humorless.

One tactic to enhance a long slide lecture is to slip in a humorous slide; say, a picture of you in a bathing suit upside down . . . Students delight in seeing their superiors out of context and it can add a personal touch to a lesson.

(9) USE HUMOR TO SYMPATHIZE WITH STUDENTS. One of the side effects of using humor is to show your students that you are human and can recognize their hardships. Saying something humorous about the bad weather, heat, the fact that it's Monday, that it's Friday, that it's early or late, is a friendly way of empathizing with students.

(10) ACKNOWLEDGE DISRUPTIONS. Most professional speakers advise you to acknowledge disruptions rather than to ignore them. Classes are often interrupted by unanticipated announcements, fire drills or noises inside and outside the room itself.

If your joke or anecdote is interrupted, you can bring your students' minds back to the joke by asking them, "Where was I?"

(11) USE HUMOR TO TEACH THE IGNORANCE BEHIND PREJUDICE. Most of what is behind the humor of ethnic and sexist jokes is unconscious hostility, prejudice and ignorance. Explaining what's behind these jokes can help teach students to understand the invalidity of stereotypes, where they come from and what their function is. Analyzing ethnic humor is one way to expose prejudice and educate students about the age, ethnic, or sexist stereotypes of American or foreign cultures.

(12) END CLASS WITH A JOKE. By planning a joke at the end of class, students can leave in a more positive mood and associate the learning experience with a good time. End jokes should be completed before the bell rings since it not only signals the end of a class but also signals the end of student listening time.

SUMMARY

Drama is an essential part of the humorous curriculum. Drama is necessary to energize and revitalize classroom learning. When students are excited about learning, they seek out educational experiences.

The Dartmouth method designed by John Rassias at Dartmouth College serves as a dynamic example of the benefits of integrating drama and humor into the curriculum. As a result of the Rassias Method, foreign language enrollment at Dartmouth increased substantially. More importantly, the combination of emotional experience and repetition has effectively improved retention of subject matter.

Students love drama in the classroom. Simulation experiences allow students to personalize the curriculum in a fun way. In addition, the simulation exercise promotes learning on many levels including social skills like cooperation and trust.

Creative drama is often a humorous experience which allows students to exercise their bodies (with pantomime) and imaginations (with improvisation, arts and crafts). Creative drama is an outlet which can supplement student performance requirements over and above oral and written requirements.

Whether or not humor is integrated into the curriculum in dramatic or non-dramatic ways, there are many opportunities for laughter in the classroom.

APPENDIX A

SELECTED TEACHER/SCHOOL FILMS
(In chronological order)

1927 — College
      (Buster Keaton)
1930 — All Quiet on the Western Front
1931 — Pardon Us.
      (Oliver and Hardy and Harry Langdon)
1932 — Horse Feathers
      (The Marx Brothers; written by S. J. Perelman)

Our Gang Series: (Featuring "Miss Crabtree")

1931 — Teacher's Pet
1932 — Readin' and Writin'
1936 — Spooky Hooky
1936 — Two Too Young

1936 — These Three
1939 — Goodbye Mr. Chips
1939 — Huckleberry Finn
      (Mickey Rooney)
1951 — Bedtime for Bonzo
      (Ronald Reagan)
1955 — Rebel Without a Cause
      (James Dean)
1958 — The Blob
      (Steve McQueen)
1958 — Teacher's Pet
      (Doris Day, Clark Gable)
1960 — Walt Disney's The Absent Minded Professor
      (Fred McMurray)

1962 — The Miracle Worker
(Anne Bancroft, Patty Duke)
1964 — Father Goose
(Cary Grant, Leslie Caron)
1966 — Who's Afraid of Virginia Wolfe
(Liz Taylor, Richard Burton)
1967 — Guess Who's Coming to Dinner
(Spencer Tracy, Katharine Hepburn, Sidney Poitier)
1968 — Rachel, Rachel
(Joanne Woodward, Estelle Parsons)
1969 — Butch Cassidy and the Sundance Kid
(Paul Newman, Robert Redford, Katherine Ross)
1969 — Good-bye Mr. Chips (remake)
1973 — The Paper Chase
(John Houseman)
1974 — National Lampoon's Animal House
(John Belushi, Donald Sutherland)
1974 — Young Frankenstein
(Gene Wilder, Marty Feldman, Madeline Kahn, Peter Boyle,
Gene Hackman)
1977 — Looking for Mr. Goodbar
(Diane Keaton)
1978 — Halloween
(Jamie Lee Curtis)
1979 — Rock and Roll High
(Mary Woronov, Paul Bartel)
1979 — All Quiet on the Western Front (remake)
1979 — Starting Over
(Burt Reynolds, Jill Clayburgh)
1980 — Altered States
(William Hert, Blair Brown)
1981 — Porky's
1981 — Prom Night
(Leslie Nielson)
1981 — Raiders of the Lost Ark
(Harrison Ford)
1982 — Fast Times at Ridgemont High
(Ray Walston, Sean Penn)
1982 — National Lampoon's Class Reunion

1982 — Pink Floyd The Wall
1983 — All the Right Moves
(Tom Cruise, Craig T. Nelson)
1983 — Class
(Jacqueline Bisset, Rob Lowe, Cliff Robertson)
1983 — Educating Rita
(Michael Caine, Julie Walters)
1983 — Porky's II
1983 — Risky Business
(Tom Cruise, Rebecca De Mornay)
1983 — Terms of Endearment
(Shirley MacLaine, Debra Winger, Jack Nicholson)
1984 — Angel
1984 — Ghostbusters
(Bill Murray, Dan Aykroyd, Sigourney Weaver)
1984 — Indiana Jones and the Temple of Doom
(Harrison Ford)
1984 — The Nerds
1984 — Oxford Blues
(Rob Lowe)
1984 — Sixteen Candles
(Molly Ringwald)
1984 — Teachers
(Judd Hirsch, Nick Nolte, Jo Beth Williams, Ralph Macchio)
1985 — Gotcha
1985 — Just One of the Guys
1985 — Porky's Revenge
1985 — Real Genius
1985 — Vision Quest
1986 — Back to the Future
(Michael J. Fox)
1986 — The Breakfast Club
(Molly Ringwald, Emilio Estevez, Ally Sheedy, Judd Nelson,
Anthony Michael Hall, Paul Gleason)
1986 — Ferris Bueller's Day Off
1986 — Back to School
(Rodney Dangerfield, Sally Kellerman)
1986 — Sweet Liberty
(Alan Alda)

APPENDIX B

SAMPLE HUMOR LIBRARY

A HUMOR LIBRARY is compiled according to the needs of the teacher and students. In addition to helpful references on public speaking and comedy techniques listed in the bibliography for Chapter Seven, teachers will want to include a few titles from each of the sections listed below. Reference texts on the background of humor offer helpful overviews on the history of humor as well as providing ideas about popular sources of the laughable.

Activity books and joke collections especially designed for the classroom are helpful sources of joke ideas. In some cases, teachers can collect joke books on specific subjects such as medicine, business, law, science, music and foreign languages. General joke anthologies usually provide hundreds or thousands of jokes or anecdotes which can be rewritten and personalized as discussed in Chapter Seven.

BACKGROUND INFORMATION

Ellenbogen, Glenn C.: *The Director of Humor Magazines and Humor Organizations in America (and Canada)*. New York, Wry-Bred Press, 1985.

Bier, Jesse: *The Rise and Fall of American Humor*. New York, Holt, Rinehart & Winston, 1968.

Blair, Walter and Hill, Hamlin: *America's Humor. From Poor Richard to Doonesbury*. Oxford, Oxford University Press, 1978.

Franklin, Joe: *Encyclopedia of Comedians*. New York, Bell, 1985.

Rourke, C.: *American Humor: A Study of National Character*. New York, Harcourt, Brace, 1971.

ACTIVITY BOOKS

Johnson, June: *838 Ways to Amuse a Child*. New York, Gramercy, 1960.

Kamiya, A.: *Elementary Teacher's Handbook of Indoor and Outdoor Games*. Englewood Cliffs, N.J. Prentice Hall, 1985.

Mathson, P.: *Creative Learning Activities for Religious Education: A Catalog of Teaching Ideas for Church, School, and Home.* Englewood Cliffs, N.J., Prentice-Hall, 1984.

Michener, Dorothy and Muschlitz, Beverly: *Filling the Gaps. A Year's Supply of Activities to Help You Survive Those Unplanned Moments.* Nashville, Tenn., Incentive, 1983.

Nelson, Patty: *Teacher's Bag of Tricks. 101 Instant Lessons for Classroom Fun!* Nashville, Tenn., Incentive, 1986.

Newmann, Dana: *The New Teacher's Almanack. Practical Ideas for Every Day of the School Year.* 2nd ed. West Nyack, N.Y., The Center for Applied Research in Education, 1980.

SCHOOL HUMOR

Baker, Sheena: *There's A Worm in my Apple.* Toronto, Stoddart, 1985.

Birnbach, Lisa: *The Official Preppy Handbook.* New York, Workman, 1980.

"Campus Comedy," in *Reader's Digest.*

Cerf, Christopher and Navasky, Victor: *The Experts Speak. The Definitive Compendium of Authoritative Misinformation.* New York, Pantheon, 1984.

Egan, Robert: *From Here to Fraternity.* New York, Bantam, 1985.

Graham, Lawrence & Hamdan, Lawrence: *F.L.Y.E.R.S. Fun Loving Youth En Route to Success. How to Remain Oblivious to the Arms Race, the Budget Deficit, Acid Rain and other Current Events that Could Put a Damper on your Bright Future.* New York, Simon & Schuster, 1985.

Highlights for Children, 2300 W. 5th Avenue, Columbus, Ohio, 43272-0002.

Kelly, Kate, David, Richard, and Stone, Jeff: *What Color Is Your Toothbrush? Or The Joys of Roommate Living.* New York, Pocket Books, 1985.

Mordden, Ethan: *Smarts. The Cultural I.Q. Test.* New York, McGraw-Hill, 1984.

Peterson, Art: *Teachers. A Survival Guide for the Grownup in the Classroom.* New York, New American Library, 1985.

Schulz, Charles M.: *Things I've Had to Learn Over and Over and Over (Plus a Few Minor Discoveries).* New York, Holt, Rinehart and Winston, 1984.

Susan, P. and Mamehak, S.: *Encyclopedia of School Humor: Icebreakers, Classics, Stories, Puns, Roasts for all Occasions.* Englewood Cliffs, N.J., Prentice-Hall, 1986.

Wilde, Larry: *The Official Smart Kids/Dumb Parents Joke Book; MORE The Official Smart Kids/Dumb Parents Joke Book; The Last Official Smart Kids Joke Book.* New York, Bantam.

SUBJECT HUMOR

Fisk, Jim and Barron, Robert: *The Official MBA Handbook or How to Succeed in Business Without a Harvard MBA.* New York, Simon & Schuster, 1982.

———— : *The Official MBA Dictionary.* New York, Simon & Schuster, 1983.

Lowry, Linda Ridge: *Humor in Instrumental Music: A Discussion of Musical Affect, Psychological Concepts of Humor and Identification of Musical Humor.* Unpublished doctoral dissertation, Ohio State University, 1974.

Robinson, Vera M.: *Humor & the Health Professions.* Thorofare, N.J. Charles B. Slack, 1977.

Trudeau, G.B.: *Adjectives Will Cost You Extra. Selected Cartoons from He's Never Heard of You, Either,* Vol. I. New York, Ballantine, 1983.

Weller, Tom: *Science Made Stupid: How to Discomprehend the World Around Us.* Boston, Houghton Mifflin, 1985.

White, D. Robert, Esq.: *The Official Lawyer's Handbook.* New York, Simon & Schuster, 1983.

———— : White's Law Dictionary. New York, Warner Books, 1985.

Wilde, Larry: *The Official Doctors Jokebook; The Official Lawyers Joke Book,* New York, Bantam.

Young, Ruth and Rose, Mitchell: *To Grill a Mockingbird and Other Tasty Titles.* New York, Viking Penguin, 1985.

FOREIGN LANGUAGE SOURCES

Ballesteros, Octavio A.: Mexican Proverbs: The Philosophy, Wisdom and Humor of a People, 1979. ED #228012.

Claire, Elizabeth: *What's So Funny? (A Foreign Student's Introduction to American Humor).* Rochelle Park, N.J., Eardley, 1984.

Editors of Passport Books: *The Insult Dictionary. How to Give 'Em Hell in Five Nasty Languages.* (French, German, Spanish, Italian, English). Skokie, Ill., National Textbook Company, 1983.

———— : *The Lover's Dictionary. How to be Amorous in Five Delectable Languages.* (French, German, Spanish, Italian, English). Skokie, Ill., National Textbook Company, 1983.

Genevieve: *Merde! The REAL French You Were Never Taught at School.* New York, Atheneum, 1986.

GENERAL SOURCES

Richler, Mordecai (Ed.): *The Best of Modern Humor.* New York, Knopf, 1983.

Adams, A.K.: *The Home Book of Humorous Quotations.* New York, Dodd, Mead, 1969.

Asimov, Isaac: *Treasury of Humor: A Lifetime Collection of Favorite Jokes, Anecdotes, and Notes on How to Tell Them and Why.* Boston, Houghton Mifflin, 1971.

Bernhard, Edgar: *Speakers on the Spot: A Treasury of Anecdotes for Coping with Sticky Situations.* West Nyack, N.Y., Parker, 1977.

Bonham, Tal D.: *The Treasury of Clean Teenage Jokes.* Nashville, Tenn., Broadman, 1985.

Brandreth, Gyles: *871 Famous Last Words and Put-downs, Insults, Squelches, Compliments, Rejoinders, Epigrams and Epitaphs of Famous People.* New York, Bell, 1979.

Brown, Marshall (Ed.): *Wit and Humor of Well-Known Quotations.* Ann Arbor, Mich., Gryphon Books, 1971.

Davis, Hal: *Laugh! A Handbook of Jokes.* Destin, Florida, Emerald Coast Publishing, 1986.

Esar, Evan: *20,000 Quips and Quotes.* Garden City, N.Y., Doubleday, 1968.

Fuller, Edmund (Ed.): *4,800 Wise-Cracks, Witty Remarks and Epigrams for All Occasions.* New York, Avenel, 1980.

———— : *2,500 Anecdotes for All Occasions.* New York, Avenel, 1980.

Lake, Antony B.: *A Pleasury of Witticisms & Word Play. A Collection of Immortal Wit, Whimsical Verse and other Literary Tours de Force.* New York, Bramhall House, 1975.

Lieberman, Gerald F.: *3,500 Good Jokes for Speakers*. New York, Doubleday, 1975.

McKenzie, E.C.: *14,000 Quips & Quotes for Writers & Speakers*. New York, Crown, 1980.

Meiers, Mildred and Knapp, Jack: *5,600 Jokes for All Occasions*. New York, Avenel, 1980.

Murphy, Edward F.: *2,715 One-Line Quotations for Speakers, Writers & Reconteurs*. New York, Crown, 1981.

———— : *The Crown Treasury of Relevant Quotations*. New York, Crown, 1978. 2nd ed., *Webster's Treasury of Relevant Quotations*. New York, Greenwich House, 1978.

Orben, Robert: *The Joke Teller's Handbook or 1,999 Belly Laughs*, 1966; *2,000 New Laughs for Speakers: The Ad-Libber's Handbook*, 1969; *The Encyclopedia of One-Liner Comedy*, 1971; *2,500 Jokes to Start 'Em Laughing, 2,100 Laughs for All Occasions*, Garden City, New York, Doubleday, 1969.

Untermeyer, Louis: *Treasury of Great Humor; Including Wit, Whimsy and Satire from the Remote Past to the Present*. New York, McGraw Hill, 1972.

Wells, Carolyn: *A Whimsey Anthology*. New York, Dover, 1976.

REFERENCES

CHAPTER ONE
A SURVEY OF EDUCATION-BASED HUMOR

Batiuk, Tom: *Funky Winkerbean.* New York, Fawcett Columbine, 1984.

Blair, Walter and Hill, Hamlin: *America's Humor. From Poor Richard to Doonesbury.* Oxford, Oxford University Press, 1978.

Breathed, Berke: *Bloom County.* Boston, Little, Brown and Co., 1983.

Bryant, Jennings and Others: Relationship between college teachers' use of humor in the classroom and students' evaluations of their teachers. *Journal of Educational Psychology,* LXXII, 4: 511-19, 1980.

Caruso, Virginia M. Teacher enthusiasm behaviors reported by teachers and students, 1982. ED #217038.

Corey, Gerald F.: *Teachers Can Make a Difference.* Columbus, Ohio, Merrill, 1973.

Dawson, Peter: *Teachers and Teaching.* Oxford: Basil Blackwell, 1984.

Detorie, Rick: *Catholics. An Unauthorized, Unapproved, Illustrated Guide.* New York, Perigee, 1986.

Highet, G.: *The Anatomy of Satire.* Princeton, Princeton University Press, 1962.

Hodgart, M.: *Satire.* New York, McGraw-Hill, 1969.

Holliday, C. *The Wit and Humor of Colonial Days.* 2nd ed. New York, Ungar, 1970.

Keillor, Garrison: School. In his *Lake Wobegon Days.* New York, Viking Penguin, 1985, pp. 169-87.

Knowlton, Bill: *Classroom Capers.* New York, Berkley, 1961; *Classroom Chuckles* (1968; *More Classroom Chuckles* (1973); *The Most in Classroom Chuckles* (1975). New York, Scholastic Book Services.

Larson, Gary: Various titles including *In Search of the Far Side,* (1980); *Beyond the Far Side,* (1983); *Valley of the Far Side* (1985); *It Came From the Far Side* (1986). Kansas City, Andrews, McMeel & Parker.

MacNelly, Jeff: *The Greatest Shoe on Earth.* New York, Holt, Rinehart and Winston, 1984.

Mandel, Howie. Going to school. *Fits Like a Glove.* Warner Brothers Records, 1986.

Mayer, Frederick: *The Great Teachers.* New York, Citadel Press, 1967.

Mitchell-Dwyer, Barbi: Are we gonna do anything fun? *English Journal,* LXX, 6: 24-25, 1981.

Mogavero, Donald T.: It's confirmed. J-students like humor in the classroom. *Journalism Educator,* XXXIV, 1: 43-44, 52-53, 1979.

Morales, Gil.: *Wake Me When the Semester's Over.* New York, Ballantine, 1983.

Neusner, Jacob: *How to Grade Your Professors and Other Unexpected Advice.* Boston, Beacon Press, 1984.

New York Magazine: *The New Yorker Album of Drawings.* 1925-1975. New York, Penguin, 1975.

Schulz, Charles M.: Various titles including *My Anxieties Have Anxieties,* (1977); *The Way of the Fussbudget Is Not Easy,* (1984); *Things I've Had to Learn Over and Over and Over (Plus a Few Minor Discoveries),* (1984). New York, Holt, Rinehart and Winston.

Tamborini, Ron and Zillmann, Dolf: College students' perception of lecturers using humor. *Perceptual and Motor Skills,* LII, 2: 417-32, 1981.

Trueblood, E.: *The Humor of Christ.* New York, Harper & Row, 1964.

Webster, G.: *Laughter in the Bible.* St. Louis, Bethany, 1960.

Woehlk, Heinz D.: Some humor in the Bible. ED #203388.

CHAPTER TWO

THE MEANING OF LAUGHTER: ITS VALUE AND FUNCTION IN THE CLASSROOM

Apte, Mahadev L.: *Humor and Laughter: An Anthropological Approach.* Ithaca and London, Cornell University Press, 1985.

Averill, J.R.: Autonomic response patterns during sadness and mirth. *Psychophysiology,* 5: 399-414, 1969.

Babad, E.Y.: A multi-method approach to the assessment of humor: A critical look at humor tests. *Journal of Personality,* 42: 618-31, 1974.

Barrie, A.: The importance of NOT being earnest. *Good Housekeeping,* LXXII, 164: 165, 1975.

Bryant, Jennings and Others: Humorous illustrations in textbooks: effects on information acquisition, appeal, persuasibility and motivation, 1980. ED #196 071.

_____ : Effects of humorous illustrations in college textbooks. *Human Communication Research,* VIII, 1: 43-57, 1981.

Damico, Sandra Bowman: What's funny about a crisis? Clowns in the classroom. *Contemporary Education,* LI, 3: 131-34, 1980.

Desberg, Peter and Others: The effect of humor on retention of lecture material, 1981. ED #223 118.

Eastman, Max: *The Sense of Humor.* New York, Scribners, 1921.

_____ : *Enjoyment of Laughter.* New York, Simon and Shuster, 1937.

Emerson, J.P.: Negotiating the serious import of humor. *Sociometry,* 32: 169-81, 1969.

Fadiman, C.: Humor as a weapon. *Journal of Creative Behavior,* 6: 87-92, 1972.

Fry, W.F. Jr.: Laughter: Is it the best medicine? *Stanford M.D.,* 10: 16-20, 1971.

_____ and P.E. Stoft: Mirth and oxygen saturation levels of peripheral blood. *Psychotherapy and Psychosomatics,* 19: 76-84, 1971.

Gruner, C.R.: *Understanding Laughter: The Workings of Wit and Humor.* Chicago, Nelson-Hall, 1978.

_____ and Dwight L. Freshley: Retention of lecture items reinforced with humorous and non-humorous exemplary material. 1979. ED #193 725.

Kaplan, Robert M. and Gregory C. Pascoe: Humorous lectures and humorous examples: some effects upon comprehension and retention. *Journal of Educational Psychology,* LXIX, 1: 61-65, 1977.

Larson, Greg: Humorous teaching makes serious learning. *Teaching English in the Two-Year College,* VIII, 3: 197-99, 1982.

Lewis, Florence C.: Self-abuse as a teaching device. *Phi Delta Kappan,* LVII, 8: 433-34, 1976.

Mettee, D.R., E.S. Hrelec and P.C. Wilkens: Humor as an interpersonal asset and liability. *Journal of Social Psychology,* 85: 51-64, 1971.

Mindess, Harvey: *Laughter and Liberation.* Los Angeles, Nash, 1971.

_____ : The limits of laughter. *Humanist,* XXXXIII, 4: 27-29, 40, 1983.

Munn, William C. and Gruner, Charles R.: Sick jokes, speaker sex, and informative speech. *Southern Speech Communication Journal,* XXXXVI, 4: 411-18, 1981.

O'Connell, W.E.: The humor of the gallows. *Omega,* 1: 31-32, 1966.

_____ : Humor and death. *Psychological Reports,* 22: 391-402, 1968.

_____ : Humour for actualization and survival, 1976. ED #137 644.

Peter, Dr. Laurence J. and Bill Dana: *The Laughter Prescription. How to Achieve Health, Happiness, and Peace of Mind Through Humor.* New York, Ballantine, 1982.

Plessner, Helmuth: *Laughing and Crying.* Churchill, James Spencer and Grene, Marjorie (Trans.): Evanston, Ill: Northwestern University Press, 1970.

Szasz, Suzanne: *The Body Language of Children.* New York, W.W. Norton, 1978.

Taylor, P.M.: The effectiveness of humor in informative speaking. *Central States Speech Journal,* 15: 295-96, 1964.

Woods, Peter: Coping at school through humor. *British Journal of Sociology of Education,* IV, 2: 111-24, 1983.

CHAPTER THREE

THE DEVELOPMENT OF A SENSE OF HUMOR

Bower, T.G.R.: *Development in Infancy.* 2nd ed. San Francisco, W.H. Freeman, 1982.

Canzler, Lillian: Humor and the primary child, 1980. ED #191 583.

Chapman, A.J.: Humorous laughter in children. *Journal of Personality and Social Psychology,* 31: 42-49, 1975.

Chukovsky, K.: *From Two to Five.* Rev. ed. Berkeley, University of California Press, 1968.

Cleary, Beverly: The laughter of children. *Horn Book Magazine,* LVIII, 5: 555-64, 1982.

Geller, Linda Gibson: Children's humorous language in the classroom, 1981. ED #203323.

Greenfield, P.M.: Playing peekaboo with a four-month-old: A study of the role of speech and nonspeech sounds in the formation of a visual schema. *Journal of Psychology,* 82: 287-98, 1972.

Groch, A.S.: Joking and appreciation of humor in nursery school children. *Child Development*, 45: 1098-1102, 1974.

McGhee, P.E.: Development of the humor response: A review of the literature. *Psychological Bulletin*, 76: 328-48, 1971.

_____ : *Humor: Its Origin and Development*. San Francisco, Freeman, 1979.

_____ and Chapman, A.J.: *Children's Humor*. London, Wiley, 1980.

McNamara, Shelley G.: Responses of fourth and seventh grade students to satire as reflected in selected contemporary picture books, 1981. ED #208402.

Prentice, N.M. and Fathman, R.E.: Joking riddles: A developmental index of children's humor. *Developmental Psychology*, 11: 210-16, 1975.

Ransohoff, Rita: Some observations on humor and laughter in young adolescent girls. *Journal of Youth and Adolescence*, IV, 2: 155-70, 1975.

Rothbart, M.K.: Laughter in young children. *Psychological Bulletin*, 80: 247-56, 1973.

Schaier, A.H. and Cicirelli, V.C.: Age changes in humor comprehension and appreciation. *Journal of Gerontology*, 31: 577-82, 1976.

Shor, R.E.: Production and judgment of smile magnitude. *Journal of Genetic Psychology*, 98: 79-82, 1978.

Shultz, T.R.: Development of the appreciation of riddles. *Child Development*, 45: 100-105, 1974.

_____ and Horibe, F.: Development of the appreciation of verbal jokes. *Developmental Psychology*, 10: 13-20, 1974.

Sroufe, L.A. and Wunsch, J.P.: The development of laughter in the first year of life. *Child Development*, 43: 1326-44, 1972.

Wendelin, Karla Hawkins: Taking stock of children's preferences in humorous literature. *Reading Psychology*, II, 1: 34-41, 1980.

CHAPTER FOUR

WHY DO WE LAUGH? THE PSYCHOLOGY OF HUMOR

Anderson, J.R.: *Cognitive Psychology and Its Implications*. 2nd ed. San Francisco, W.H. Freeman, 1985.

Brodzinsky, D.M. and Rightmeyer, J.: Pleasure associated with cognitive mastery as related to children's conceptual tempo. *Child Development*, 47: 881-84, 1976.

Berger, A.A.: What makes people laugh? *ETC*, 32: 427-28, 1975.

Chapman, Antony J. and Foot, Hugh C. (Eds.): *Humour and Laughter: Theory, Research and Applications*. London, John Wiley & Sons, 1976.

_____ (Eds.): *It's a Funny Thing, Humour*. Oxford, Pergamon, 1977.

Clark, M.: Humour and incongruity. *Philosophy: Journal of the Royal Institute of Philosophy*, 45: 20-32, 1970.

Cunningham, A.: Relation of sense of humor to intelligence. *Journal of Social Psychology*, 57: 143-47, 1962.

Darwin, Charles: *The Expression of Emotions in Man and Animals*. 1st ed. London, John Murray, 1872.

Deckers, L. and Kizer, P.: Humor and the incongruity hypothesis. *The Journal of Psychology*, 90: 215-18, 1975.

Freud, Sigmund: *Wit and Its Relation to the Unconscious*. London, T.F. Unwin, 1916.

———— : Humour. *The International Journal of Psychoanalysis*, 9: 1-6, 1928.

Fromkin, V.A.: Slips of the tongue. *Scientific American*, CCXXIX, 6: 110-17, 1973.

Giles, H. and Oxford, G.S.: Towards a multidimensional theory of laughter causation and its social implications. *Bulletin of the British Psychological Society*, 23: 97-105, 1970.

Goldstein, Jeffrey H.: Humor appreciation and time to respond. *Psychological Resports*, 27: 445-46, 1970.

———— : Theoretical notes on humor. Laughing Matter? A Symposium of Studies on Humor as Communication. *Journal of Communication*, XXVI, 3: 104-112, 1976.

Harter, S.: "Pleasure derived by children from cognitive challenge and mastery." *Child Development*, 45: 661-69, 1974.

———— , T.R. Shultz and B. Blum: Smiling in children as a function of their sense of mastery. *Journal of Experimental Child Psychology*, 12: 396-404, 1971.

Hassett, J. and Houlihan, J.: Different jokes for different folks. *Psychology Today*, 12: 64-71, 1979.

Jung, C.G.: On the psychology of the trickster figure. In *The Trickster*, Radin, Paul, (Ed.). New York, Schocken Books, 1956, pp. 195-211.

Kreitler, H. and Kreitler, S.: Dependence of laughter on cognitive strategies. *Merrill-Palmer Quarterly*, 16: 163-77, 1970.

Lee, J.C. and Griffith, R.M.: Forgetting jokes: A function of repression? *Journal of Individual Psychology*, 19: 213-15, 1963.

Legman, Gershon: *Rationale of the Dirty Joke: An Analysis of Sexual Humor*. New York, Grove, 1968.

———— : *No Laughing Matter: Rationale of the Dirty Joke, Second Series*, Bloomington, IN, Indiana Univ. Press, 1982.

Levine, Jacob and Redlich, Fred C.: Intellectual and emotional factors in the appreciation of humor. *Journal of Genetic Psychology*, 62: 25-35, 1960.

Lewis, M. and Goldberg, S.: The acquisition and violation of expectancy: An experimental paradigm. *Journal of Experimental Child Psychology*, 7: 70-79, 1969.

Maier, N.R.F.: A gestalt theory of humor. *British Journal of Psychology*, 23: 69-74, 1932.

Maw, W.H. and Maw, E.W.: Differences between high- and low-curiosity fifth-grade children in the recognition of verbal absurdities. *Journal of Educational Psychology*, LXIII, 6: 558-62, 1972.

McGhee, Paul E. and Goldstein, Jeffery H. (Eds): *The Psychology of Humor*. New York, Academic Press, 1972.

———— (Eds.): *The Handbook of Humor Research*. New York, Springer, 1983.

McGhee, P.E. and Johnson, S.F.: The role of fantasy and reality cues in children's appreciation of incongruity humor. *Merrill-Palmer Quarterly*, 21: 19-30, 1975.

McGhee, Paul E. and Lloyd, Sally A.: A developmental test of the disposition theory of humor. *Child Development*, 52: 925-31, 1981.

Muthayya, B.C. and Mallikarjunan, M.: A measure of humour and its relation to intelligence. *Journal of Psychological Researches*, 13: 101-105, 1969.

O'Connell, Walter: Multidimensional investigation of Freudian humor. *Psychiatric Quarterly*, 38: 97-108, 1964.

_____ and Peterson, P.: Humor and repression. *Journal of Existential Psychiatry*, 4: 309-316, 1964.

Perlett, Robert: What's so funny? — Sigmund Freud to the rescue. *English Journal*, LXXI, 4: 60-62, 1982.

Piaget, Jean: *The Psychology of Intelligence*. Piercy, Malcolm and D.E. Berlyne, (Trans.) Totowa, N.J.: Littlefield, Adams, 1976.

Pien, D. and Rothbart, M.K.: Incongruity and resolution in children's humor: A reexamination. *Child Development*, 47: 966-71, 1976.

Pollio, H.R. and Mers, R.W.: Predictability and the appreciation of comedy. *Bulletin of Psychonomic Society*, 4: 229-32, 1974.

Redlich, F.C.: Intellectual and emotional factors in appreciation of humor. *Journal of General Psychology*, 62: 25-35, 1960.

Rosenbaum, R.J.: *Toward a Symbolic Theory of Humor: A Jungian Perspective*. Unpublished Doctoral Dissertation, California School of Professional Psychology, San Diego, 1976.

Schmidt, N.E. and Williams, D.I.: The evolution of theories of humor. *Journal of Behavioral Science*. 1: 95-106, 1971.

Shultz, T.R.: The role of incongruity and resolution in children's appreciation of cartoon humor. *Journal of Experimental Child Psychology*, 13: 456-77, 1972.

Shurcliff, A.: Judged humor, arousal, and the relief theory. *Journal of Personality and Social Psychology*, 8: 360-63, 1968.

Sinnott, J.D. and Ross, B.M.: Comparison of aggression and incongruity as factors in children's judgments of humor. *Journal of Genetic Psychology*, 128: 241-49, 1976.

Svebak, S.: Three attitude dimensions of sense of humor as predictors of laughter. *Scandinavian Journal of Psychology*, 15: 185-90, 1975.

Terry, R.L. and Ertel, S.L.: Exploration of individual differences in preferences for humor. *Psychological Reports*, 34: 1031-37, 1974.

Thomas, D.R., Shea, J.D. and Rigby, R.G.: Conservatism and response to sexual humour. *British Journal of Social and Clinical Psychology*, 10: 185-86, 1971.

Treadwell, Y.: Humor and creativity. *Psychological Reports*, 26: 55-58, 1970.

Turk, Edward Baron: Comedy and psychoanalysis: The verbal component. *Philosophy & Rhetoric*, 12: 95-113, 1979.

Verinis, J.S.: Inhibition of humor enjoyment: Effects of sexual content and introversion-extroversion. *Psychological Reports*, 26: 167-70, 1970.

Whitt, J.K. and Prentice, N.M.: Cognitive processes in the development of children's enjoyment and comprehension of joking riddles. *Developmental Psychology*, 13: 129-36, 1977.

Williams, C. and Cole, D.L.: The influence of experimentally induced inadequacy feelings upon the appreciation of humor. *Journal of Social Psychology*, 64: 113-17, 1964.

Wilson, G.D. and Patterson, J.R.: Conservatism as a predictor of humor preferences. *Journal of Consulting and Clinical Psychology*, 33: 271-74, 1969.

Wolosin, R.J.: Cognitive similarity and group laughter. *Journal of Personal and Social Psychology*, 32: 503-509, 1975.

Woolfolk, Anita E. and McCune-Nicolich, Lorraine: *Educational Psychology for Teachers*. 2nd ed. Englewood Cliffs, N.J., Prentice-Hall, 1984.

Zigler, E., Levine, J. and Gould, L.: Cognitive challenge as a factor in children's humor appreciation. *Journal of Personality and Social Psychology*, 6: 332-36, 1967.

Ziv, Avner: The influence of humorous atmosphere on divergent thinking. *Contemporary Educational Psychology*, VIII, 1: 68-75, 1983.

——— : *Personality and the Sense of Humor.* New York, Springer, 1984.

CHAPTER FIVE

THE SOCIAL DYNAMICS OF LAUGHTER

Askenasy, G.H.: Humor: Aggression, defense, and conservatism. Group characteristics and differential humor appreciation. *Social Behavior and Personality*, 4: 75-80, 1976.

Broadhead, R.S.: Notes on the sociology of the absurd. *Pacific Sociological Review*, 17: 35-46, 1974.

Brodzinsky, David M. and Others: Sex of subject and gender identity as factors in humor appreciation. *Sex Roles: A Journal of Research*, VII, 5: 561-73, 1981.

Bruner, J.S., Jolly, A. and Sylva, K. (Eds.): *Play: Its Role in Development and Evolution*. New York, Basic Books, 1976.

Cantor, Joanne R.: What is funny to whom? The role of gender. Laughing Matter. *Journal of Communication*, XXVI, 3: 159-67, 1976.

Chapman, A.J.: Social facilitation of laughter in children. *Journal of Experimental Social Psychology*, IX, 6: 528-41, 1973.

Cottrell, N.B.: Performance in the presence of other human beings: Mere presence, audience and affiliation effects. In E.C. Simmel, R.A. Hoppe and G.A. Milton (Eds.), *Social Facilitation and Imitative Behavior.* Boston, Allyn & Bacon, 1968.

Dabbs, J.: Physical closeness and negative feelings. *Psychonomic Science*, 23: 141-43, 1971.

Davis, J.M. and Farina, A.: Humor appreciation as social communication. *Journal of Personality and Social Psychology*, 15: 175-78, 1970.

Eakins, B.W. and Eakins, R.G.: *Sex Differences in Human Communication.* Boston, Houghton Mifflin, 1978.

Emde, R.N., Gaensbau, T.S. and Harmon, R.J.: Social smiling and a new level of organization. *Psychological Issues*, X, 1, Monograph 37: 86-93, 1976.

Felker, D.W. and Hunter, D.M.: Sex and age differences in response to cartoons depicting subjects of different ages and sex. *Journal of Psychology*, 76: 19-21, 1970.

Fink, E.L. and Walker, B.A.: Humorous responses to embarrassment. *Psychological Reports*, 40: 475-85, 1977.

Foot, H.C., Smith, J. and Chapman, A.J.: Boys and girls come out to play: Sex differences in social interaction of young children. *New Behaviour*, 1: 418-20, 1975.

Fox, G.: 'Nice girl': Social control of women through value construct. *Signs*, II, 4: 805-17, 1977.

Fuller, R.G.C. and Sheehy-Skeffington, A.: Effects of group laughter on responses to humourous material: A replication and extension. *Psychological Reports,* 35: 531-34, 1974.

Garvey, C.: *Play.* Cambridge, Mass, Harvard University Press, 1977.

Goldstein, Jeffrey H.: *Sports, Games, and Play: Social and Psychological Viewpoints.* Hillsdale, N.J., L. Erlbaum Associates, 1979.

Goodchilds, J.D.: Effects of being witty on position in the social structure of a small group. *Sociometry,* 22: 261-72, 1959.

Goodlad, S.: On the Social Significance of Television Comedy. Bigsby, C.W. (Ed.): *Approaches to Popular Culture.* London, Edward Arnold, 1976.

Grote, B. and Gvetkovitch, G.: Humor appreciation and issue involvement. *Psychonomic Science,* 27: 199-200, 1972.

Grotjahn, Martin: Laughter and sex. *Human Sexuality,* 3: 92-96, 1969.

_____ : Sexuality and humor: Don't laugh. *Psychology Today,* 6: 50-53, 1972.

Hertzler, Joyce O. *Laughter. A socio-Scientific Analysis.* New York, Exposition, 1970.

Howells, Kevin (Ed.): *The Psychology of Sexual Diversity.* Oxford, New York, Basil Blackwell, 1984.

Leventhal, Howard and Cupchik, Gerald C.: The informational and facilitative effects of an audience upon expression and the evaluation of humorous stimuli. *Journal of Experimental Social Psychology,* 11: 363-80, 1975.

Levine, J.: Humor and play in sports. In R. Slovenko & J.A. Knight (Eds.) *Motivation in Play, Games and Sports.* Springfield, Illinois, Thomas, 1967.

Levinson, R.M.: From Olive Oyl to Sweet Polly Purebread: Sex role stereotypes and television cartoons. *Journal of Popular Culture,* IX, 3: 561-72, 1975.

Lieberman, J. Nina: *Playfulness. Its Relationship to Imagination and Creativity.* New York, Academic Press, 1977.

Lindzey, Gardner and Aronson, Elliott: *The Handbook of Social Psychology,* 2nd ed. Cambridge, Mass., Addison-Wesley, 1969.

Losco, J. and Epstein, S.: Humor preference as a subtle measure of attitudes toward the same and the opposite sex. *Journal of Personality,* 43: 321-34, 1975.

Lundberg, C.: Person-focused joking: Pattern and function. *Human Organization,* 28: 22-28, 1969.

McGhee, Paul E.: Development of children's ability to create the joking relationship. *Child Development,* 45: 552-56, 1974.

_____ : Sex differences in children's humor. *Journal of Communication,* XXVI, 3: 1976.

O'Connell, W.E.: The social aspects of wit and humor. *Journal of Social Psychology,* 79: 183-87, 1969.

Piaget, Jean: *Play, Dreams and Imitation in Childhood.* New York, W.W. Norton, 1962.

Piddington, Ralph: *The Psychology of Laughter: A Study in Social Adaptation.* 2nd ed. New York, Gamut, 1963.

Pollio, Howard R. and Bainum, Charlene Kubo: Are funny groups good at solving problems? A methodological evaluation and some preliminary results. *Small Group Behavior:* XIV, 4: 379-404, 1983.

Prerost, Frank J.: The effects of high spatial density on humor appreciation: Age and sex differences. *Social Behavior and Personality,* VIII, 2: 239-44, 1980.

———— and Brewer, Robert E.: The appreciation of humor by males and females during conditions of crowding experimentally induced. *Psychology: A Quarterly Journal of Human Behavior,* XVII, No. 1: 15-17, 1980.

Priest, R.F.: Sexism, intergroup conflict and joking. *JSAS/Catalogue of Selected Documents in Psychology,* 2: 15, 1972.

Radcliffe-Brown, A.R.: On joking relationships. *Africa,* 13: 195-210, 1940.

———— : A further note on joking relationships. *Africa,* 19: 133-40, 1949.

Ruben, Harvey L.: *Competing.* New York, Pinnacle, 1981.

Sherman, L.W.: An ecological study of glee in small groups of preschool children. *Child Development,* 46: 53-61, 1975.

Stephenson, R.M.: Conflict and control functions of humor. *American Journal of Sociology,* LVI, 6: 569-74, 1951.

Sternglanz, S.H. and Serbin, L.A.: Sex role stereotyping in children's television programs. *Developmental Psychology,* 10: 710-15, 1974.

Suls, J.M.: The role of familiarity in the appreciation of humor. *Journal of Personality,* 43: 335-45, 1975.

Whiting, B.B. and Edwards, C.P.: A cross-cultural analysis of sex differences in the behavior of children aged three through eleven. *Journal of Social Psychology,* 91: 171-88, 1973.

Wilson, G.D., Nias, D.K.B. and Brazendale, A.H.: Vital statistics. Perceived sexual attractiveness and response to risque humor. *The Journal of Social Psychology,* 95: 201-205, 1975.

Wilson, W.: Sex differences in response to obscenities and bawdy humor. *Psychological Reports,* 37: 1074, 1975.

Winick, Charles: The social contexts of humor. Laughing Matter? *Journal of Communications,* XXVI, 3: 124-28, 1976.

Winn, Marie: The plug-in generation. *Change,* III, 17: 14-20, 1985.

Worthen, R. and O'Connell, W.E.: Social interest and humor. *International Journal of Social Psychiatry,* 15: 179-88, 1969.

Wyer, R.S., Weatherley, D.A. and Terrell, G.: Social role, aggression and academic achievement. *Journal of Personality and Social Psychology,* 1: 645-49, 1965.

Zillman, D.: Retaliatory equity as a factor in humor appreciation. *Journal of Experimental Social Psychology,* 10: 480-88, 1974.

Zippin, D.: Sex differences and the sense of humor. *Psychoanalytic Review:* 53: 209-19, 1966.

CHAPTER SIX

THE ROLE OF LANGUAGE IN HUMOROUS STRUCTURES

Ayoub, M. and Barnett, S.A.: Ritualized verbal insults in white school culture. *Journal of American Folklore,* 78: 337-44, 1965.

Bateson: The position of humor in human communication. Levine, M.T. (Ed.): *Motivation in Humor.* New York, Atherton, 1969, pp. 159-66.

Berger, A.A.: Anatomy of the joke. *Journal of Communication,* XXVI: 113-15, 1976.

Bowles, Colin: *Wit's Dictionary.* London, Angus & Robertson, 1984.

Brandreth, Gyles: *The Joy of Lex. How to Have Fun with 860,341,500 Words.* New York, Quill, 1983.

Briden, Earl F.: The jargonist as comedian: An approach to usage. *ABCA Bulletin,* XXXXV, 1: 39-41, 1982.

Buffington, Perry W. Slipping up. *Sky,* December: 105-106, 108, 1986.

Douglas, Mary: 'Jokes' and 'do dogs laugh?' A cross-cultural approach to body symbolism. *Implicit Meanings: Essays in Anthropology,* London, Routledge & Kegan Paul, 1975, pp. 83-89 and 90-114.

Dubois, Barbara R.: I've got it badly and that ain't well. *English Journal,* LXXIII, 4: 46-47, 1984.

Geller, Linda Gibson: Children's humorous language in the classroom. ED #203323.

Gillespie, Tim: Lampooning language. *English Journal,* LXXI, 3: 65-69, 1982.

Holmes, Glyn: The humorist in the language laboratory. *Modern Language Journal,* LXIV, 2: 197-202, 1980.

Hughes, Patrick: *More on Oxymoron. Foolish Wisdom in Words and Pictures.* Middlesex, England, Penguin Books, 1983.

Jackson, R.W.: *The Diabolical Dictionary of Modern English.* New York, Delacorte, 1986.

Kirshenblatt-Gimblett, B. (Ed.): *Speech Play.* Philadelphia, University of Pennsylvania, 1976.

Legman, Gershon: *The New Limerick.* New York, Crown, 1977.

Lehr, Fran: ERIC/RCS: Promoting vocabulary development. *Journal of Reading,* XXVII, 7: 656-58, 1984.

Mencken, H.L.: *The American Language.* 4th ed. New York, Alfred A. Knopf, 1985.

Nilsen, Alleen Pace: Children's multiple uses of oral language play. *Language Arts,* LX, 2: 194-201, 1983.

Rasking, Victor: *Semantic Mechanisms of Humor.* Boston, D. Reidel, 1984.

Schultz, Thomas R. and Pilon, R.: Development of the ability to detect linguistic ambiguity. *Child Development,* 44: 728-33, 1973.

Tibbetts, S.: What's so funny? Humor in children's literature. *California Journal of Educational Research,* 24: 42-46, 1973.

Tyson, Eleanore S. and Mountain, Lee: A riddle of pun makes learning words fun. *Reading Teacher,* XXXVI, 2: 170-73, 1982.

Wilson, Christopher P.: Jokes: Form, content, use and function. European Monographs in Social Psychology, 16. *Social Research,* 35: 286-311, 1968. And New York, Academic, 1979.

Zillmann, D. and S.H.: Putdown humor. *Journal of Communication,* 26: 154-63, 1976.

CHAPTER SEVEN

THE TEACHER AS ENTERTAINER: COMIC TECHNIQUE IN THE CLASSROOM

Adams, Richard C.: Is physics a laughing matter? The Physics Teacher, May: 265-66, 1972.

Berry, Gordon L.: *Strategies for Successful Teaching in Urban Schools: Ideas and Techniques from Central City Teachers.* Palo Alto, Calif., R & E Research Associates, 1982.

Gray, Jenny: *The Teacher's Survival Guide. How to Teach Teenagers and Live to Tell About It.* Palo Alto, Calif., Fearon, 1967.

Greenberg, Herbert M.: *Teaching with Feeling. Compassion and Self-Awareness in the Classroom Today.* Toronto, Macmillan, 1969.

Hegarty, Edward J.: *Humor and Eloquence in Public Speaking.* West Nyack, New York, Parker, 1976.

Helitzer, Melvin: *Comedy Techniques for Writers and Performers.* Athens, Ohio, Lawhead Press, 1984.

_____ : *Comedy Writing Secrets. How to Think Funny, Write Funny, Act Funny, and Get Paid for It.* Cincinnati, Ohio, Writer's Digest Books, 1987.

Hillman, Bill W.: *Teaching with Confidence. How to Get Off the Classroom Wall.* Springfield, Illinois, Thomas, 1981.

Johnson, Eric W.: *Teaching School. Points Picked Up.* Boston, National Association of Independent Schools, 1979.

Keene, Melvin: *Beginning Secondary School Teacher's Guide.* New York, Harper & Row, 1969.

Kenny, Michael F.: *Presenting Yourself.* New York, John Wiley & Sons, 1982.

Lax. E.: *On Being Funny.* New York, Charterhouse, 1975.

Lessinger, Leon M.: *Teaching as a Performing Art.* Dallas, Crescendo, 1976.

Maley, Alan: *Drama Techniques in Language Learning.* New York, Cambridge University Press, 1978.

Martin Maggs, Margaret: *The Classroom Survival Book. A Practical Manual for Teachers.* New York, New Viewpoints, 1980.

Nelson, Robert B.: *Louder and Funnier. A Practical Guide for Overcoming Stagefright in Speechmaking.* Berkeley, California, Ten Speed Press, 1985.

Peacher, Georgiana: *Speak to Win. A Complete Guide to Making Your Voice More Powerful, Pleasant & Effective.* New York, Bell, 1985.

Perret, Gene: *How to Write & Sell Your Sense of Humor.* Cincinnati, Ohio, Writer's Digest Books, 1982.

_____ : *How to Hold Your Audience with Humor. A Guide to More Effective Speaking.* Cincinnati, Ohio, Writer's Digest Books, 1984.

Saks, Sol: *The Craft of Comedy Writing.* Cincinnati, Ohio, Writer's Digest Books, 1985.

Salutin, M.: The impression management techniques of the burlesque comedian. *Sociological Inquiry,* 43: 159-68, 1973.

Simmons, Sylvia H.: *How to Be the Life of the Podium.* New York, AMACOM, 1982.

Smith, Terry C.: *Making Successful Presentations.* New York, John Wiley & Sons, 1984.

Smuin, Stephen K.: *Turn-Ons! 185 Strategies for the Secondary Classroom.* Belmont, Calif., David S. Lake, 1978.

Wilde, Larry: *How the Great Comedy Writers Create Laughter.* Chicago, Nelson-Hall, 1976.

CHAPTER EIGHT
HUMOR AND TEST ANXIETY

Alpert, Richard and Haber, Ralph Norman: Anxiety in academic achievement situations. *Journal of Abnormal and Social Psychology,* LXI, 2: 207-15, 1960.

Brown, Alan S. and Itzig, Jerry M.: The interaction of humor and anxiety in academic test situations, 1976. ED #152783.

Cohen, Ruth I.: Reducing test anxiety: A right brain approach, 1980. ED #3190966.

Ehrlich, Eugene: *How to Study Better and Get Higher Marks.* 2nd rev. ed., New York, Thomas Y. Crowell Co., 1976.

Erwin, Bette and Dinwiddie, Elza Teresa: *Test Without Trauma. How to Overcome Test Anxiety and Score Higher on Every Test.* New York, Grosset & Dunlap, 1983.

Graham, Lawrence: *Conquering College Life. How to be a Winner at College.* New York, Washington Square Press, 1983.

Hammes, John A. and Wiggins, Stewart L.: Manifest anxiety and appreciation of humor involving emotional content. *Perceptual and Motor Skills,* XIV: 291-94, 1962.

Hedl, John J., Jr. and Others: Test anxiety and humor appreciation, 1978. ED #163080.

Krohne, Heinz W. and Laux, Lothar, (Eds.): *Achievement, Stress, and Anxiety.* The Series in Clinical and Community Psychology. Washington, New York and London, Hemisphere Publishing Corp., 1982.

McMorris, Robert F. and Others: Effects of including humor in test items, 1983. ED #230588.

Mechanic, David: *Students Under Stress. A Study in the Social Psychology of Adaptation.* New York, The Free Press of Glencoe, 1962.

Nieves, Luis R.: *Coping in College: Successful Strategies.* Princeton, New Jersey, Educational Testing Service, 1984.

Pauk, Walter: *How to Study in College.* 3rd ed. Boston, Houghton Mifflin, 1984.

Paul, Gordon L. and Eriksen, Charles W.: Effects of test anxiety on 'real-life' examinations. *Journal of Personality,* 32: 480-94, 1964.

Rubin, Joan and Thompson, Irene: *How to Be a More Successful Language Learner.* Boston, Heinle & Heinle, 1982.

Sarason, Irwin G., Pederson, Andreas M. and Nyman, Barry: Test anxiety and the observation of models. *Journal of Personality,* 36: 493-511, 1968.

Sarason, Irwin G., (Ed.): *Test Anxiety: Theory, Research, and Applications.* Hillsdale, N.J., Lawrence Erlbaum Associates, 1980.

Sieber, Joan E., O'Neil, Harold F., Jr. and Tobias, Sigmund: (Eds.): *Anxiety, Learning, and Instruction.* Hillsdale, N.J., Lawrence Erlbaum Associates, 1977.

Smith, Ronald E. and Ascough, James C., Ettinger, Ronald F., and Nelson, Don A.: Humor, anxiety, and task performance. *Journal of Personality and Social Psychology,* XIX, 2: 243-46, 1971.

Smouse, Albert D. and Munz, David C.: The effects of anxiety and item difficulty sequence on achievement testing scores. *The Journal of Psychology,* 68: 181-84, 1968.

Spielberger, Charles D., (Ed.): *Anxiety. Current Trends and Research.* Vol. II. New York and London, Academic Press, 1972.

Terry, Roger L. and Isaacson, Randall M.: Item failure and performance on subsequent items of an achievement test. *The Journal of Psychology,* 77: 29-32, 1971.

Terry, Roger L. and Woods, Margaret E.: Effects of humor on the test performance of elementary school children. *Psychology in the Schools,* 12: 182-85, 1975.

Townsend, Michael A.R., Mahoney, Peggy and Allen, Linda G.: Student percep-
tions of verbal and cartoon humor in the test situation. *Educational Research Quarterly,* VII, 4: 17-23, 1983.

CHAPTER NINE
CLASS CLOWNS AND OTHER JOYS OF TEACHING

Anonymous: The gifted-talented-creative child may range from being completely in-
visible to being the class wit, punster-joker-clown. *Creative Child and Adult Quarterly,* I, 3: 184-86, 1976.

Bleedorn, Bernice B.: Humor as an indicator of giftedness. *Roeper Review,* IV, 4: 33-
34, 1982.

Bryant, Jennings and Others: Children's imitation of a ridiculed model. *Human Communication Research,* X, 2: 243-55, 1983.

Caspari, Irene E.: *Troublesome Children in Class.* London and Boston, Routledge and
Kegan Paul, 1976.

Clarizio, Harvey F.: *Toward Positive Classroom Discipline.* New York, John Wiley &
Sons, 1971.

Damico, Sandra Bowman and Purkey, William W.: The class clown phenomenon
among middle school students. Gainesville, Florida Educational Research and
Development Council, 1976. ED #128703.

————— : Class clowns: A study of middle school students. *American Educational Research Journal,* XV, 3: 391-98, 1978.

Deitz, Samuel M. and Hummel, John H.: *Discipline in the Schools. A Guide to Reducing
Misbehavior.* Englewood Cliffs, New Jersey, Educational Technology Publications,
1978.

Dubelle, Stanley T., Jr. and Hoffman, Carol M.: *Misbehavin'. Solving the Disciplinary
Puzzle for Educators.* Lancaster, Pa., Technomic, 1984.

Duke, Daniel Linden and Maravich Meckel, Adrienne: *Managing Student Behavior
Problems.* New York, Teachers College, Columbia University, 1980.

————— : *Teacher's Guide to Classroom Management.* New York, Random House, 1984.

Emmer, Edmund T. and Others: *Classroom Management for Elementary Teachers.* Englewood Cliffs, N.J., Prentice-Hall, 1984.

————— : *Classroom Management for Secondary Teachers.* Englewood Cliffs, N.J.,
Prentice-Hall, 1984.

Fisher, Seymour and Fisher, Rhoda Lee: *Pretend the World is Funny and Forever: A Psychological Analysis of Comedians, Clowns and Actors.* Hillsdale, N.J., L. Erlbaum Assoc.,
1981.

Gagne, Eve E.: *School Behavior and School Discipline. Coping with Deviant Behavior in the
Schools.* Washington, D.C., University Press of America, 1982.

Gallahger, Mary: Teaching comedy to class comedians. *English Journal,* LXXI, 2: 51-
52, 1982.

Goodchilds, J.D. and Smith, Ewart E.: The wit and his group. *Human Relations,* 17:
23-31, 1964.

Long, James D. and Frye, Virginia H.: *Making it till Friday. A Guide to Successful Classroom Management.* 3rd ed. Princeton, N.J., Princeton Book Co., 1985.

Nathan, D.: *The Laughtermakers.* London, Peter Owen, Ltd., 1971.

Ramsey, Robert D.: *Educator's Discipline Handbook.* West Nyack, New York, Parker, 1981.

Riginos, Alic Swift: *Platonica. The Anecdotes Concerning the Life and Writings of Plato.* Leiden, E.J. Brill, 1976.

Sirois, F.: Clownery and the child. *Acta Psychiatrica Belgica,* 73: 654-58, 1973.

Smith, E.E. Goodchilds, J.D.: Characteristics of the witty group member: The wit as leader. *American psychologist,* 14: 375-76, 1959. (Abstract).

_____ : The wit in large and small established groups. *Psychological Reports,* 13: 273-74, 1963.

Smith, E.F. and White, H.L.: Wit, creativity, and sarcasm. *Journal of Applied Psychology,* 49: 131-34, 1965.

Sperling, S.J.: On the psychodynamics of teasing. *Journal of the American psychoanalytic Association,* 1: 458-83, 1953.

Sprick, R.: *Discipline in the Secondary Classroom: A Problem-By-Problem Survival Guide.* Englewood Cliffs, N.J., Prentice-Hall, 1985.

Stocking, S.H. and Zillmann, D.: Effects of humorous disparagement of self, friend, and enemy. *Psychological Reports,* 39: 455-61, 1976.

Towsen, J.H.: *Clowns.* New York, Hawthorn Books, 1976.

Wegmann, Robert G.: Classroom discipline: A negotiable item. *Today's Education,* LXV, 3: 92-93, 1976. Reprinted in part as "Tips on discipline." *Today's Education,* LXXI, 3: 44-45, 1982.

Welsford, Enid: *The Fool: His Social and Literary History.* London, Faber & Faber, 1968.

Willeford, William: *The Fool and His Scepter: A Study in Clowns and Jesters and Their Audience.* Evanston, Ill., Northwestern University Press, 1969.

CHAPTER TEN

HUMOR AND CREATIVE DRAMA IN THE CLASSROOM

Bacon, Richard M.: The thunder and lightning professor. *Yankee Magazine,* September: 108-113, 200-205, 1977.

Bolton, Gavin: *Drama as Education: Argument for Placing Drama at the Centre of the Curriculum.* Essex, England, Longman, 1984.

Brizendine, Nancy Hanks and Thomas, James L.: *Learning Through Dramatics: Ideas for Teachers and Librarians.* Phoenix, AZ, Oryx Press, 1982.

Byrd, Charles W., Jr.: Intensive language instruction at a small liberal arts college: The Dartmouth model at Emory & Henry. *Modern Language Journal,* LXIV, 3: 297-302, 1980.

Courtney, Richard: *The Dramatic Curriculum.* London, Ontario, Faculty of Education, University of West Ontario, 1980.

Gillis, Don: Teaching as a performing art, 1975. ED #117093.

Heck, Shirley F. and Cobes, Jon P.: *All the Classroom Is a Stage. The Creative Classroom Environment.* New York, Pergamon, 1978.

Heinig, R. and Stillwell, L.: *Creative Drama for the Classroom Teacher.* 2nd ed. Englewood Cliffs, N.J.: Prentice-Hall, 1981.

Horner, Jeanne and Stansfield, Charles: The Dartmouth/Rassias Method: An Annotated bibliography, 1980. ED #181716.

James, Ronald. *A Guide to Improvisation: A Handbook for Teachers.* Banbury, England, Kemble Press, 1980.

Kelly, Elizabeth Elory: *Dramatics in the Classroom: Making Lessons Come Alive.* Bloomington, Indiana, Phi Delta Kappa Educational Foundation, 1976.

LaZere, Sonia. What's new and fun? The Dartmouth foreign language method. *PEALS,* 18: 20-21, 1978.

Lessinger, Leon M.: *Teaching as a Performing Art.* Dallas, Crescendo, 1976.

Luxenberg, Stan: All the class a stage, Intensive language instruction. *Change* 3: 30-33, 1978.

Maley, Alan and Duff, Alan: *Drama Techniques in Language Learning.* New York, Cambridge University Press, 1978.

McCaslin, Nellie: *Creative Drama in the Classroom.* 4th ed. New York, Longman, 1984.

Nighbert, Esther: *Today Let's Improvise: A Handbook on Creative Dramatics for Teachers and Leaders.* Johnstown, Pa., Mafex Associates, 1976.

Sloyer, Shirlee: *Readers Theatre: Story Dramatization in the Classroom.* Urbana, Ill.: National Council of Teachers of English, 1982.

Smith, Stephen M. *The Theater Arts and the Teaching of Second Languages.* Reading, Mass., Addison-Wesley, 1984.

Stanley, Susan M. *Drama Without Script: The Practice of Improvised Drama.* London, Hodder and Stoughton, 1980.

Stewig, John W.: *Informal Drama in the Elementary Language Arts Program.* New York, Teacher's College, Columbia University, 1983.

Watkins, Beverly T.: Will using drama to teach languages lure more students to the classroom? *The Chronicle of Higher Education,* January 7: 3, 1980.

DATE DUE